Along Came a Leader

A Guide to Personal and Professional Leadership at Any Age

Kelly Croy

Along Came a Leader
A Guide to Personal and Professional Leadership at Any Age

Kelly Croy

A Walnut Street Book
Published by Walnut Street Publications

Published by Walnut Street Publications
Toledo, Ohio

For ordering information or special bulk purchases please contact: Kelly Croy 218 East Main Street Oak Harbor, Ohio 43449 1-800-831-4825

ISBN-13: 978-1512393064

ISBN-10: 1512393061

"*Kelly Croy brings his perspective as a leader and an educator to inspire you to make more of your opportunities for impact. This is a thoughtful book written by a leader who has learned his insights in the classroom of life.*"

Mark Sanborn, Author of *The Fred Factor*, **a Wall Street Journal, Business Week and New York Times bestseller.**

•••

"*Kelly Croy is a leader in every sense of the word. He has been leading lives for as long as I can remember. He is a teacher, motivator, coach and leadership guru. When he talks I listen and when he writes I take note. Kelly is not only one of the most gifted communicators that I know but one of the most inspirational individuals I know.*

In this new book, Kelly notes that leadership is both lovely and lonely. It can be isolated at the top but he reminds us that it doesn't have to be. True leadership is not only marching forward but reaching back to pour into others. True leadership is selfless not selfish and Kelly has not only a way with words but this concept down and we are all better for him sharing. Those whom lead must read and this is one book that you absolutely must get for your library to glean from again and again. Buy one for yourself and TWO to give away!"

Frank Shelton, Author of *Final Approach* **and** *Carrying Greatness*

*"The true meaning of life is to plant trees,
under whose shade you do not expect to sit."*

~Nelson Henderson

This book is dedicated to my father,
Richard Keith Croy

Contents

Introduction 1

CHAPTER 1: Do You Really Want to be a Leader? 7

CHAPTER 2: What is Leadership? 9

CHAPTER 3: Everyone is Called to Lead 14

CHAPTER 4: Attitude 20

CHAPTER 5: Wisdom 47

CHAPTER 6: Tenacity 77

CHAPTER 7: Communication 113

CHAPTER 8: Vision 155

CHAPTER 9: Authenticity 179

Leadership Takes Courage 205

The Six Leadership Commitments 207

About the Author 211

Acknowledgements 213

Quotes on Leadership 219

Leadership Maxims 225

Introduction

I have found the writing of a book, which this is my first, to be a most difficult challenge. It's not so much the writing of it, but the abandoning of it that is the hardest. There is no exact recipe for a book, nor a timer to chime when it's finished. When does an author know to stop? For me, no such recognition ever came. I simply decided it was time to move on to another project, as the subject of leadership could be discussed for a lifetime. I have not tried to approach every facet of leadership, for that would be incredibly confusing and prove quite unproductive. Rather, I have attempted to distill leadership into manageable concepts that one could practice and improve upon, and to create a tool from which one can benefit, use, and pass on to others.

These were my guiding goals.

Leadership to me is not a talent nor birthright, but rather a skill to be practiced, honed, and mastered. It is my hope to have contributed to this craft and art of leadership with the writing of this work.

A wise man once told me, "No one has an opinion until you announce your's." I have found these words to be incredibly true during the researching and writing of this book on leadership. Many have shared their opinions, insight, and even admonishments.

I imagine this book to have several types of readers: Some will read it in hopes to prove their claim to a leadership position. Others will approach it with much curiosity and bias as to what qualifies me to write a book on leadership. Some will read with a red pen, identifying grammatical errors, of which they will be sure to find. Finally, some will read it to understand leadership concepts and improve themselves as leaders. It is for this latter group that I write.

What compels someone to write a book on leadership? For me, that question was answered rather easily; I wanted to help others become better leaders.

> *"The best way to become acquainted with a subject is to write a book about it."*
> **~ Benjamin Disraeli**

Parents want their children to be leaders. Teachers want leaders in their classrooms. Coaches want their teams to be filled with leaders. Employers want to hire leaders. Churches are waiting for leaders to emerge. Communities and local governments desperately need leaders.

The problem is that each person and organization is expecting each other to take care of the training. Parents want the schools to do it. Schools expect the parents to do it. Soon one can identify a problematic loop: everyone wants a leader, everyone agrees they are important, but no one is quite sure where they originate, nor wishes to spend the time in shaping one.

It is with this problem that I began researching and writing about leadership. I have shared my observations and findings on stage as a speaker, in the locker room and on the field as a coach, at home as a parent, and within business corporations as a consultant. Leadership matters and it can be taught.

> *"Leadership doesn't just make a difference, leadership is the difference."*
> **~Mark Sanborn**

Leadership is the deciding factor in the success of people, organizations, relationships, and of any endeavor worthy of an investment of time and resources. So where are these leaders the world so desperately needs?

The world is waiting for leaders to arrive. So, **Along Came A Leader** seemed to be the natural fit for a title.

"Let us think of education as the means of developing our greatest abilities, because in each of us there is a private hope and dream which, fulfilled can be translated into benefit for everyone and greater strength for our nation."
~ **John F. Kennedy**

Apple Computers was at the brink of complete and utter failure when Dell Computers CEO, Michael Dell, announced what he would do if he were the CEO of Apple, "What would I do? I'd shut it down and give the money back to the shareholders."

And then... Along Came a Leader. Steve Jobs and his **vision** turned Apple into the greatest company on the planet. Apple changed the world again and again with the iPod, the iPhone, and a continuous stream of innovations.

•••

During World War II Great Britain was on the brink of being overtaken. London was being bombed regularly. The Home Guard, comprised of citizens, was organized to delay an imminent German invasion.

And then... Along Came a Leader. Winston Churchill led his country with **tenacity** and away from the clutches of Adolf Hitler with the rallying cry of never surrendering.

•••

In 1996 Marvel Comics went bankrupt. The comic book giant had little hope of recovery. Readership was falling rapidly.

And then... Along Came a Leader. First, Isaac Perlmutter's **wisdom** merged the comic giant with his Toy Biz, Inc. and grew the company's stock prices and cash flow through licensing for media and products. Then, Avi Arad **wisely** secured a massive line of credit for Marvel to begin making its own movies. Marvel now makes the big-screen blockbuster everyone wants to see and is a huge corporate success.

•••

The darkest chapters of American history are those of our nation's struggles for civil rights. From the earliest days of our nation's founding to the 1960s and beyond, Americans have been denied the right to eat, learn, work, and live with other Americans based on the color of their skin, religious beliefs, and gender.

And then… Along Came a Leader. Martin Luther King's ability to **communicate** the vision of a world of harmony opened the eyes to the possibilities for our great nation. His words continue to inspire, free, and change the destinies of people around the world long after his death. He peacefully fought for the civil liberties of all people.

•••

The people of South Africa suffered from the social afflictions of apartheid for decades. Apartheid divided the country with a wound so deep it seemed unable to be healed. The nation began tilting toward decline and was viewed by many as irreversible.

And then… Along Came a Leader. Nelson Mandela and his tremendous **attitude** of optimism and compassion unified the region in ways most believed unimaginable. Even after over twenty years of imprisonment Nelson Mandela was able to maintain an attitude so positive he didn't even harbor vindictive thoughts toward his former captors. He was elected president of the region, made incredible reforms, and is loved by many around the world for his compassionate attitude.

•••

Calcutta, India was a city of great juxtaposition. In Calcutta you could find both the poorest of the poor, and the wealthiest of the rich within incredibly short distances from one another. Sadly, for a very long time the city offered no help or hope to the dying babies and children of the poor. It would seem this poor, lowly class of people were doomed to suffer an inevitable eradication, without any assistance, and remain completely invisible to the rest of the world.

And then… Along Came a Leader. Mother Teresa left the comforts of her employment with the wealthy to attend and care for the poorest of the poor. Her **authenticity** in her leadership to remain steadfast to the values for which she took an oath and devoted her life, brought help to this region and its plight, and made it visible to the world so more aid could be sent.

•••

Leaders make the difference. **Leadership** makes a difference. Whatever problem presented, there is always a solution — leadership. Whether the problem is global, national, regional, corporate, or within our own families, or even within our own personal lives, the solution is still — leadership. It is my sincerest hope and aim that this book, **Along Came a Leader**, will inspire you to become a leader and assist you on that journey. When the next challenge is presented, whether it be within an organization, business, sports team, classroom, or your home, when the leader eventually comes along, I want it to be *you.*

One of my goals for my life is to write a book that makes a difference in someone else's life. I know books can change lives. I certainly have read a few that have changed mine for the better. It is my hope that this book can do the same for you.

I believe all books have the *potential* to change lives if we allow them. Too often though readers rush through a book. Sure, they pick up a few 'gold nuggets' that help them with their lives in some way, but only when we slow down and *own* the chapter we are reading do we allow a book to make a difference. By "owning" the chapter, I mean we personalize the examples, and we apply the lesson to specific areas within our own lives. We make the reading personal, we write in the margins, we underline, highlight, and ask questions. Please own this book and personalize your experience to get the most from it.

I struggled greatly with pronouns in the writing of this work. You will notice I will jump back and forth between "he" and "she" when talking about the roles of future leaders. I did this with the intention of having all readers feel comfortable with the text. I live with five women, my wife and four daughters. It is very important that I encourage leadership of both genders equally and encourage all to become leaders.

I hope you will send me a message after you have finished reading **Along Came a Leader** and let me know about your reading experience. You may be surprised about how I respond to messages sent to me. <u>Kelly@kellycroy.com</u>

CHAPTER 1

Do you really want to be a leader?

I hear a lot of people say leadership is important, but I cannot help but to question their sincerity. In many years of teaching and coaching, and my travels as a speaker and artist, a common theme among everyone I have come in contact is the importance of the leadership. Or so they say.

Do you really want to be a leader?

My experience says no. I think most people confuse leadership with being the star. They don't want to be a leader. They want their picture in the paper, the trophy on the mantle, or their name on the record board. They want to tell relatives that they are the captain of the team, the president of the club, and add another title to the college entrance application or professional resume. They want to be well liked and admired. That is what I believe most people want.

The truth is that while leadership can often be a truly rewarding experience, it is often a lot of hard work. Leaders have responsibilities whether their team wins or loses, whether their corporation is making a profit or hitting a rough patch, or whether their family is having the time of their life or suffering a cruel hardship. Leaders are often ridiculed and criticized, and they work well beyond 'their fair share' with little truly to show for it. Leadership is not a popularity contest and it isn't about being the star.

Do you really want to be a leader?

If you are still answering yes then I must ask you what you are doing to become a leader? Do you criticize public leaders in front of others? Complain about the decisions a leader has made? Do you volunteer in leadership roles? Do you look for and accept opportunities to make decisions and serve others? Or are you too busy?

If you want to lead you really do have to step forward. It's not going to happen on its own, and you can't expect someone to come find you and beg you to lead; you must look for opportunities to serve others. So many people assume someone else will *make them* the leader; perhaps a teacher, coach, or administrator will *choose* them to be a leader. Leadership happens long before the title is given. Seek leadership by doing more than your fair share. Get involved. Stand up. Speak up.

The ingredients we mix into a bowl determines the dish we prepare. Yes or no? You don't get cookies using spinach. What ingredients are going in you, and will they make you a leader? What books do you read? What games do you play? What do you listen to? What movies do you watch? Who do you admire? With whom do you spend your time? *These are important questions.*

I want to be a leader because I really want to make a difference in the world. I understand that our lives have purpose, and that we are here to help others accomplish great things. I understand I may be ridiculed, criticized, and beaten down. I know the decisions I make as a leader may cause me to lose friends or be unpopular. And I know when the time comes I may choose *not to lead*, but I will always be **prepared**.

Will you?

Do you really want to be a leader?

CHAPTER 2

What is leadership?

In order to become a good leader you must be able to identify good leadership.

I have seen men and women who have been elected, appointed, volunteered, and even thrust into leadership positions, that had no idea what they were suppose to do. Some mistakenly thought their job was to boss everyone else around. Others thought they were to change everything from the way the previous leader had it. Still others thought a leader was the only person that should talk or make decisions. In an age that so desperately needs great leaders, it is sad to find so few, and with that realization, the idea for this book was formed.

What qualifies someone to write a book on leadership? Do you need to be elected to a high office, manage a Fortune 500 company, or lead a team to a world championship? While those accomplishments may be excellent models of leaders, they may not always be able to verbalize the qualities of great leaders. No, the requirements and qualifications of a leader are woven into the lives of everyone that aspires to bring out the best in others. Leaders are found in the parents who raise great children, teachers that inspire students to become contributing members of society, and everywhere we find someone willing to make a difference. While I do not think a doctor must have a disease in order to treat it, nor a psychologist to be institutionalized in order to aid a patient's mental health, I am leaning on my twenty plus years of teaching and coaching, the founding of three successful entrepreneurial endeavors, parenting four incredible children, a successful marriage and years of research involved in the writing of this book, as well as all my life experiences and accomplishments. I wish to deliver to you, what I believe leaders need to seek in order to be great, so when you next hear the call to lead you are prepared.

I was fortunate to be surrounded with excellent leaders from birth. My parents taught each of their children to lead. Much of their wisdom is intertwined within the pages of this book. My parents operated a small business that also taught us the fundamentals of business leadership as well as the excitement for entrepreneurship. Leadership was something that was taught, nurtured, and encouraged in both our home and business. Leadership can and should begin early.

The ideals and principles of leadership were continued in my participation in many organizations and sports. The Boy Scouts of America and football taught me to step forward and make a difference rather than wait for someone else to do it. I was encouraged to be a man of action. I earned the Eagle Scout Rank and went on to play college football. I had a desire to lead. I was editor of a college magazine, captain of the rugby team, and a member of many collegiate organizations even while starting my first business, a t-shirt design company for campus programs and activities.

I graduated with a dual major in four years and began teaching and coaching at the age of twenty-one. Soon afterward, I had completed my Master's degree in English Literature and worked over twenty hours toward a doctorate in English Literature. I became involved in local politics and organizations, started a family, and organized an investment club, started student organizations, and founded several successful businesses. I do not share this in an attempt to impress you with my accomplishments; I share this to impress upon you that leaders are people who take action and impact lives. The life of a leader is busy and full of accomplishments, but it is not one of ease. Leaders have this innate sense of responsibility to the world, an internal desire to contribute and improve, and to create what did not exist before them.

Do you have that desire? Do you seek to lead? If so, then this book is for you.

A person can devote a lifetime to becoming an excellent leader. In this book, I will share with you the six primary elements I believe are necessary to become an influential leader.

THE SIX PRIMARY ELEMENTS OF LEADERSHIP
Attitude
Wisdom
Tenacity
Communication
Vision
Authenticity

You could spend a lifetime mastering just these six elements of leadership, but through their study you will be introduced to many new concepts and ideas to help you become a great leader. As you work to improve in one area, you will gain ground in another. You will be introduced to other leadership concepts and tactics. That is the nature of becoming a leader. You will add to your leadership library and resources, but these original six will forever serve as your foundation when answering the call to lead.

A leader is someone that makes an impact in the lives of others and encourages them to make a positive difference in the world we live. This is an important theme that will be repeated in this book. A leader is a person who sets an example for others to follow and has the ability to influence others into action. A leader does this by discovering the best in others and drawing it out of them, and guiding them to a greater life.

Leaders truly impact the lives of others. They model the way things should be done so well that others wish to follow a similar path. Leaders know the dreams of the people around them and they help make those dreams obtainable; genuine appreciation and loyalty follow. Leaders hold everyone around them to a higher level, challenging them to become their best. These secrets and so much more are found within these pages.

Leaders take action: As you begin this book, I would like to offer you the wise words I saw inscribed on the entrance of the first school at which I ever taught:

Enter to Learn; Go Forth to Serve.

You could read this book and many other excellent books on leadership from cover to cover many times, and I hope you do, but if you put none of it to action, nothing will happen. Likewise, if you put some of it to action, something will happen. Ultimately, if you put a lot of it into action, a lot will happen. Leadership is about taking action. It's not a title, a birthright, a degree, an achievement, or a status. In fact, it really shouldn't even be a noun. Leadership is an action. You are either leading or you are not. Choose to lead.

The Most Important Word of Leadership! If I could sum leadership up in a single word, it would be a difficult task, but the word I would have to choose would be ACTION.

Leaders speak when others remain silent. They stand up when others remain seated. They right the wrongs of the world, and create something that never existed before, simply because it was needed. Leaders recognize their part in the world, and understand they have a responsibility to others. They seek to serve a greater calling, and fill their life with a genuine purpose.

Leaders take action.

The most influential leaders in my life were the ones who emerged to help me when I needed it. I didn't ask. They appeared. They knew what needed to be done. Sometimes it happens in person. You meet a leader that gets you out of a difficult problem. Sometimes it's a reassuring phone call that everything is going to be okay. They share a vision of a better tomorrow. They remind you that they aren't leaving your side. They encourage you to take action. They inspire you to lead.

Leaders are willing to take a chance to make a change. They risk criticism. They understand leadership isn't a popularity contest. They 'get' that people might not appreciate what they've done, and dislike some of their words and actions, but they understand that not trying is worse. Leadership, they know, isn't really about *them*. Leadership is about making a difference. Leadership is about change.

You can possess every element of leadership I mention in this book: attitude, communication, wisdom, vision, tenacity, and authenticity, but if you don't follow it up with the final ingredient, ACTION, nothing will ever happen. Nothing.

Leaders not only hear the call to lead, they answer it.

As my friend Mark Sanborn always reminds his audiences, "Leadership doesn't just make a difference, it IS the difference."

There is one little secret that I think each and every person must know about leadership. Upon hearing it, it will forever change how one views the idea of leadership and their role in it.

The secret is, *everyone* is called to lead. At some point in their life it will be someone's turn to lead something. Will they answer the call? Will they be ready?

CHAPTER 3

Everyone is Called to Lead

Leadership roles await each of us around every corner.

Everyone receives the call to lead at some point in their life. Few are called with the sensationalism of the Bat Signal, a request from the president, or the ringing of a red phone under a glass dome, but all leaders are equally significant because all contain an opportunity to impact a life. Whether your call to leadership arrives in the form of public office, captaining a team, corporate management, serving in the Armed Forces, accepting the responsibilities of parenthood, or any of the other various community services and volunteer programs so readily available, you must be prepared and knowledgable about how to begin, execute, and prevail. This book is written for those who answer the call to lead, despite their age, despite experience, and despite whether they responded with a resounding 'Yes!' or a silent and apathetic nod. You have answered the call!

"Men make history, and not the other way around.
In periods where there is no leadership, society stands still.
Progress occurs when courageous, skillful leaders seize the
opportunity to change things for the better."
~Harry Truman

Leaders are not born, but made. The call to lead rings in the ear of every man and woman, but only a few have the courage to answer, and even fewer have the knowledge to execute the role well. I believe people want to be good leaders. I believe people have an earnest desire to perform the duties of leadership to the best of their ability. The problem of our lack of strong leaders is that little is being done to produce great leaders.

The mural in my high school weight room read "Champions are Made not Born." Is the same true of leaders?

Some time ago, a friend of mine asserted the notion to me that leaders are born with *that something special* that makes them so. He really is a leader, so I gave the matter some thought.

The answer came easily. He was right! Leaders are born.

Yep. It's that simple. Leaders really are born with that *special something* that enables them to influence others and accomplish something for the greater good. There is no question about it.

But here's the catch...

Without question, each and every one of us are born to lead. Yep, every one of us is born with that special something to lead others. One hundred out of every hundred have it. The problem is that 99 out of every hundred don't know how to awaken it, summon it, or call it to action. That special something lies dormant and undiscovered.

There are times and certain situations that kindle that leader within. The eighteen year old Marine in Afghanistan that nine months earlier wouldn't raise his hand in math class becomes a leader under the pressure and circumstances of war. The high school football player that didn't talk once during the season, steps forward to speak at his end of the year award's banquet to inspire underclassman to avoid the temptations of alcohol and drugs. More often than not, however, men and women will not be confronted with the circumstances that activate their internal leader, but when and if they do, training and experience become of the utmost significance. Couldn't a leader become even a better leader through experience, training, role models, influence, and practice? Absolutely.

The books we read, the people we meet and the challenges we take on matter. Leadership is not reserved for just those holding political office or dominating the boardrooms of corporations. Leaders are those brave enough to raise a family, teach a class, volunteer for community service, coach a sports team, start a carpool, petition for a better community, write a letter to the editor, and more. The call to lead resonates in everyone brave enough to answer it, and strive to make our world better.

I have taught and coached for a long time, and I have heard a common request by parents, teachers, and coaches alike; we need more leaders. They recognize that leadership makes a difference in our homes, schools, and communities. Unfortunately each believes the other is doing what is necessary to help forge our future leaders.

Leadership is a resource that cannot be taken for granted, and it certainly won't be solved by a population boom.

Each of us needs to take real measures to insure that those we can influence, are being influenced. Do not rely on others to make certain leadership is at the forefront of our schools, athletics, politics, and families. Become involved. Support leadership programs that challenge our youth. Make books and other quality resources on leadership readily available to those within your industry and home. And most importantly, serve as a positive leadership role model for others and discuss what qualities you believe make a strong leader and how they can be obtained.

For my part, I will continue to write and speak about leadership to anyone that will read or listen. I am convinced of its worth and its ability to make a difference. My dream is to share my art and words with as many people in my lifetime as possible. We may never know what impact we will have, but we will certainly know what impact we will have if we do nothing. I will not be faulted for inaction. I will always attempt to make a difference.

What is a leader? A leader is someone that speaks up when others are silent, stands up when everyone else remains seated, and has an internal drive to make a positive difference in the world. A leader is someone that sees others for their best and knows how to draw that from them. A leader has the ability to make a difference.

When do we lead? Your time as leader doesn't really begin at the point you agreed to take the role. It isn't your election, appointment, or volunteering hand that initiated your term as *leader*. No, your leadership began way before that. It isn't the title, but the actions of the individual that make the leader. You were selected, appointed, or elected because you had already started to establish yourself as a leader in smaller circles and certain events. Your actions and efforts have been recognized and now validated with a title. And the secret only a few people understand is that we are *always* leading.

You're not too young, nor too old to lead.

There is no age limit on leadership. You can accomplish anything you want at any age. We sometimes limit ourselves by believing that we will get around to doing certain things later on in life. The simple truth of the matter is that we must start *now*. Sure we might get better at it over time, but if we do not begin, it will never happen.

There also is no magic age at which the rite of leadership is bestowed. With the right combination of the leadership characteristics outlined in this book even young voices will command attention and lead others to great accomplishments.

While age carries experience, youth quite often brings energy. Both are powerful allies in the quest to lead. Lean on your strengths. Don't be defined by labels.

There is a leader within you.

I hear people all the time tell me that they simply are not leaders. It baffles me. That simply is not true. We are all called to lead. You either step forward or you do not. Tough times forge leaders! Circumstances sometimes bring out the leadership capabilities within us. If you are questioning yourself as a leader, fear not, this book will serve as an excellent assistant and comfort. You are a leader.

I have worked with leaders with speech impediments, physical challenges, and every shape, size, and disposition. There is no cookie-cutter, one-size-fits-all mold that we can pour ourselves into. By mastering the six elements outlined in this book, however, and putting what we have learned to action we can become the type of leader we were destined to become and the leader our circumstances request.

It's time to step forward and answer the call to lead.

Unleash the Leader Within.

So what do you need to do to unleash the leader within you? It's simple: 1) learn as much about leadership as you can 2) identify and model successful leaders in history, and 3) put what you learn to action. In this book, six defining leadership traits are examined to help you on your journey of becoming the leader you want to become. For now, *knowing* that you *are* a leader is enough. I am talking about confidence. Leaders must have and exhibit confidence. I'm not talking arrogance, but truly you need to let yourself and others know that you are capable of making a tremendous impact in the people you are about to lead. You may counsel with others, organize meetings, even take polls and votes at times, but in the end you are the person making the decision. When a batter steps up to the plate he is playing for the entire team, but he is the one taking the swings. Use this book to unleash the leader that already dwells within you.

You Cannot Fail.

If it's not you, then who? If you do not rise up and lead then the job goes to someone else. That's fine, as long as you trust that person making the decisions and calling the shots. I like to lead because I know, along with everyone else around me, that I am going to give my absolute best at all times. I am not going to accept failure. Failure arrives when you stop trying, and I won't stop trying until there is progress. The same is true for you. Keep at it, until something happens. You cannot fail, unless you quit trying.

Everyone at some point in their life is called to lead, and everyone, regardless of their title or position is indeed a leader. There is much to learn about leadership, but one ingredient is king of all leadership traits, and the next chapter is devoted entirely to its mastery --- attitude.

CHAPTER 4

Attitude

A good attitude is the most important element in leadership. Period.

Even if you acquired and mastered all of the other qualities outlined in this book, yet failed to develop a good attitude, you will fail as a leader. Furthermore, if you possessed only adequate measures of the other traits mentioned in this book, yet nurtured a fantastic attitude, you will excel as a leader. Yes, your attitude is indeed that important! To put it quite simply, your attitude will make you, or break you as a leader.

> *"Attitude is a little thing that makes a big difference."*
> ~ **Winston Churchill**

I was a football coach for many years. One year during two-a-days one of our seniors became extremely disappointed that he was not voted captain of the team. I sat with him for a few minutes and listened. He explained, and accurately, that he had good grades, was a talented athlete, had been with the program a long time, and would do a great job. I had no argument with what he told me; all was true. I asked him why he thought the other athletes didn't vote him as captain. He fell silent for quite awhile. I waited. Finally, he admitted to me he knew it wasn't about popularity, because he was probably more popular than the three boys selected as captains, he knew the others just didn't see him as a leader, yet. He explained that his teammates loved to joke around with him, but they could just never see him as a leader. He admitted that at the time, the way he lived was mostly about himself. He was a fabulous athlete in individual sports, but he lacked the attitude needed to be the captain of the football team. In short, he had the wrong attitude for the job. I was amazed at his honesty and his straightforwardness. He would someday make a fine leader.

"So now what?" he asked. "It's my senior year and I'm not the captain of the football team. I've dreamt of this my entire life."

I looked him in the eye and told him, "We are all captains."

Leadership isn't about titles and positions of authority. Leadership is about taking a specific action at the needed moment. Any of us can be leaders at any time. In fact, we all should be leading.

Without a doubt, this young man mustered the right attitude for the remainder of the season and clearly became the leader the other members of the team looked up to as the athlete leading them to battle each week. He changed his attitude, and changed his direction. By the end of the season he was actually recognized for his leadership, and captained another sport that year.

The young man could have hung his head low and been sad that he was not voted captain, but that wouldn't have helped the team. He became the most outstanding leader of the team. His attitude helped everyone! He raised the bar for the captains-elect, his fellow teammates, and the coaches. This young man's amazing attitude is still admired today, years later. In fact, he is seen by all I know as one of the best leaders to graduate from our school.

A title doesn't make you a leader, it's your attitude. Make the choice to lead regardless if you are the captain, the president, or holder of office. Choose to lead.

My friend Mark Sanborn is a bestselling author and an amazing public speaker. He has expanded this important principle into an incredible book titled, *You Don't Need a Title to Be a Leader: How Anyone, Anywhere, Can Make a Difference.* You really should give it a read.

It will make a difference in your life and others.

For years a banner hung in my classroom that read: '**Attitudes are contagious. Is your's worth catching?**' It was one of my favorite posters because it packed so much into one small saying. I learned right away as a teacher and coach that my students and athletes would mirror my attitude. If I arrived with an enthusiastic spirit willing to learn, so would they. If I was short tempered and impatient, well, they would mirror that as well. It's no surprise then in the work place or in sports that people mirror the attitudes of their leaders, whether they are the manager of a company, the team captain of a sports team, the classroom teacher, or a parent leading a home. Attitudes are mirrored.

Poems are a powerful way to illustrate a point with great emotion. My brother mailed the following poem to me my first year playing college football. I guess he wanted me to be a positive role model and leader to his son, my nephew Zach, and other young men. The words impacted me on the first reading. I kept it laminated and on my desk throughout college, and eventually committed it to memory. It passes through my mind often. I share it now with you:

Little Eyes Upon You

There are little eyes upon you and they're watching night and day.

There are little ears that quickly take in every word you say.

There are little hands all eager to do anything you do; And a little boy who's dreaming of the day he'll be like you.

You're the little fellow's idol, you're the wisest of the wise. In his little mind about you no suspicions ever rise.

He believes in you devoutly, holds all you say and do; He will say and do, in your way when he's grown up just like you.

There's a wide-eyed little fellow who believes you're always right; and his eyes are always opened, and he watches day and night.

You are setting an example every day in all you do; For the little boy who's waiting to grow up to be like you.

~Anonymous

Time and time again I have thought back to that poem's wisdom. When we are in leadership positions people look up to us in many ways, and we must work to set a great example. That example begins and ends with our attitude. More often than not we are unaware of those that are looking up to us, and it is for those reasons we must be extra careful. We must always check our attitude.

Attitude is a Choice

If you made a list of qualities that you did not admire and absolutely didn't want any part, they might closely resemble: laziness, stubbornness, bossiness, selfishness, snobbiness, etc. And really, what are each of these, but nothing more than a poor attitude? I tell you again, change your attitude and you will change your destiny. Keep a great attitude and you will lead.

The quality that we most admire in others has much to do with their attitude as well. We love to be around people who are pleasant, support our dreams, are confident, relaxed under pressure, and take the time to listen. These too are traits of a good attitude. Our attitude as a leader is what attracts and repels.

Leadership is about influencing others. We cannot influence those who don't want to be around us or listen to us. Our attitude is what draws them toward us and the goals we wish to achieve.

Regardless of where your attitude is now, you can change and improve upon it. The change can come immediately and have permanence in your life. There is always time to become a better you. A person can shed five pounds of fat and become a bit more fit. Likewise, a person can identify a few flaws in their attitude and adjust them for the better. Both take a little work, but provide tremendous results. Truly, a small effort will go a long way.

A good leader is someone that is always adjusting their attitude. Just like a golfer is making fine adjustments to his swing, a lineman adjusting his stance, and a writer tweaking her prose, a leader continuously makes attitude adjustments. Leaders reflect on how they work with others, spot weak points in attitude and correct them. These adjustments make them appealing. Their appeal offers them the ability to influence, and that is what makes them a strong leader.

Charles Swindoll understood the importance of attitude and worded it best when he said, "Attitude, to me, is more important than facts. It is more important than the past, than education, than money, than circumstances, than failures, than successes, than what other people think or say or do. It is more important than appearance, giftedness or skill. It will make or break a company, a church, or a home. The remarkable thing is that we have a choice every day regarding the attitude we will embrace for that day." Swindoll's words are as true today as they were when he first penned them. Attitudes are paramount.

A great attitude is simply a matter of choice. Yes, we have a choice. I choose my attitude and so do you. To say you can't help it, or that it's the result of circumstances is untrue. We choose our reaction to everything that happens in our life. We assign what meaning it has to us. We control how we allow it to influence our interactions with others. Your attitude is a choice. Can the leader of our country allow the circumstances of his morning breakfast to impact his attitude with his decision making of the day and how he treats world leaders? No. He chooses not to allow it to influence his attitude. He moves beyond it. He focuses on maintaining a good and positive attitude.

There are simple techniques and methods we can employ to achieve the attractive attitude of a leader. It's not imitation; it's change. Devoting yourself to acquiring a better attitude is devoting yourself to becoming a better leader.

Flintstone Vitamins

A good attitude is the Flintstone Vitamin of leadership; it automatically boosts all of the other leadership elements. A great attitude can compensate and even overcome a deficiency in another area. If you are a poor communicator, for example, that will hinder your ability to lead, but if your attitude is great, it will automatically boost your ability to communicate, and get you through some rough patches until you are able to strengthen you communication skills.

My mom always set out a Flintstone Vitamin for me in the morning. (I always wanted Dino. He seemed to have a lot of energy.) I remember mom explaining to me the importance of taking the vitamin every day and how it would help me in math class, and football practice, in art class, and even playing with my friends. I can't help but to think of our attitudes acting in exactly the same way. Whatever I am doing, a great attitude will make me even better at it. Make sure you take your great attitude with you everywhere you go. Like the vitamin, work on it daily. Don't skip.

Imagine you had to work beside one of two people who were equally skilled, but one had a better attitude. Who would you choose to work with? With whom would you want to date of those two equally attractive choices? Have perform dental work on you? And the list goes on. The winner? No surprise is it? We will always choose the person with the better attitude, and more often than not, even when they are inferior in other areas. Consciously or subconsciously we always choose to spend time with and follow people with winning attitudes.

Apply the same choice to leadership. Who would you follow? The answer is the same. We are attracted to positive attitudes.

Just like the Flintstone Vitamin, we can choose to take on a good attitude or not. It is our choice. When poor circumstances or misfortune come our way we can choose to get negative and hot-headed, or place our thoughts on a new direction. Choosing to have a good attitude is not being fake either. It's being mature. It's telling yourself that there are circumstances more important than you. Check your attitude by reminding yourself it's not about you.

Servant Leadership

The best leaders in my opinion are the ones that have adopted the leadership philosophy of a servant leader. They're the leaders that are never too busy to help, and never above any job. They are respected by everyone. They make great decisions because they really know what's going on within their organization. They take care of everyone within an organization.

The term servant leader was first coined in the 1970s by Robert Greenleaf, and inspired by great leaders such as Martin Luther King and many others.

> *"Good leaders must first become good servants."*
> **~Robert Greenleaf**

A servant leader does not place himself above others and boss others around. A servant leader does just what the term implies; he serves. A servant leader sees his role as a worker, serving the needs of others first. A servant leader doesn't see the others in the organization as working for him, he sees himself as leading them by serving their needs.

A servant leader sets the example with his actions. His primary focus is to personally see to the needs of others. As a servant leader walks down the hallway of his organization he picks up the paper off the floor as he walks. He looks for any area small or large to offer a hand. No aspect is too small or large. This creates both engagement and loyalty.

Any person that adopts and applies with sincerity the principles of servant leaders will be enchanting, genuine, and loved.

> *"The greatest discovery of my generation is that human beings can alter their lives by altering their attitudes of mind."*
> ~ **William James**

Building the Attitude of a Leader

In 2005 my wife and I attended a U2 concert in Cleveland, Ohio. Lead singer and frontman, Bono, offered some advice to the audience between sets for living a successful life. "You have to learn to walk with a little swagger," he said. He's right. A successful leader needs to develop a walk, yes a walk, that conveys confidence.

Books are judged by their covers, people are evaluated within the first thirty seconds of their interview, and leaders are indeed measured by how they carry themselves physically. Study the body language of those you admire. How we position our body impacts how others view us, but it also impacts how we behave as well.

President Barack Obama is routinely noted for the confidence he projects. He has mastered his walk. Think of the importance of our country's leader projecting confidence to not only the American people, but to members of foreign countries as well. Our attitude is visible to others by the way we stand and walk, as well as the words we speak, and actions we take.

My friend Matthew Kelly, author of *The Rhythm of Life* puts it another way, "You have to walk as if you do not have a care in the world." He encourages us, and rightfully so, to be conscious about how we carry ourselves, how we sit, how we communicate, and how we walk.

Confidence is not the same as arrogance or self-righteousness; you must be able to differentiate between them, and confidence certainly isn't about treating a problem lightly. Confidence is knowing that you care and will work hard to remedy any problem and take everyone within an organization to a better level. That's it. As leaders we need to act in a confident and reassuring manner.

An attitude of confidence is paramount in a leader. The United Kingdom's propaganda poster 'Keep Calm. Carry On' was used as a psychological reinforcement to the people of England during the bombing raids of World War II. Preparing for a possible German invasion the UK's leaders knew how easily attitudes are transferred. They wished to encourage an attitude of confidence and leadership. Others will mirror the attitude you model. How you carry yourself is a building block in creating the attitude of a leader. It is a necessity of day to day interactions with others, and confidence is especially important in times of crisis. Effective leaders use their self-confidence to reassure others.

Overconfidence, of course, can become a weakness of a leader. No one wants to be around someone arrogant. No one wants to follow someone that is boastful or believes they are never wrong. People need and want someone that can laugh at a mistake and then help to correct it. Quality is important in any job, but a leader looks at a much bigger picture than just quality. A leader focuses on service, and service is all about attitude.

Mistakes, a confident leader knows, are the necessary stops on the journey to success. A leader celebrates these mistakes and refers to them as "beta" or practice examples while edging forward to a master or gold copy. Perfection is unobtainable in any person or project. We seek progress not perfection. We want a leader that wants to grow and become better, not one that thinks he's perfect. A leader will be remembered on how he handles a mistake, rather than the number of mistakes made.

A leader must exhibit the correct attitude toward mistakes, whether they are his own or someone else's. Some mistakenly believe that admitting mistakes, asking for help, or accepting criticism, deteriorates an image of confidence but nothing could be further from the truth; when handled correctly admitting to a setback or mistake can strengthen a leader's credibility. Leaders need not to *appear* authentic, they need to be authentic. If a leader attempts to hide his mistake, then those following will be 'taught' that they should hide their mistakes as well. The attitude and actions of the leader will always be mirrored.

A leader of course cannot be called a leader until he has been tested and challenged by hard times, made a difficult decision, and ultimately persevered and advanced his organization. A person can be given a title or a position of leadership, but circumstances become the litmus test to whether someone is truly a leader. We build confidence with every choice we make, and the more challenging the situation the greater the mandate.

*"You can begin to shape your own destiny by
the attitude that you keep."*
~ Michael Beckwith

If people recognize you as a leader and accept you as a leader it is in large part due to your ability to project confidence and the attractive attitude that surrounds you. It's not the stripes on your uniform, nor the title alongside your name, but rather, the attitude you bring with you during good times and bad. It's easy to lead when all is well. Real leaders emerge when problems arise.

Remind Yourself: You are the Leader for the job! There are times when you may question yourself as a leader. Don't fret it. A little inner reflection and questioning is healthy. This internal evaluation is a great time to pause and take note of why you wish to lead and how you will be effective.

Here's a helpful activity: Make a list of all of your strengths, resources, and qualities that make you a good leader and the right person. Use your journal if you have one. Be creative and thorough. This is not the time to weight or list areas you need to improve upon and make improvements. No, that will come later. Right now make a list of what you have to offer. What leadership qualities do you possess? Heck, just the notion that you care and want to make a difference will make you stand out from most. Make that list now!

This list will add to your confidence and overall attitude. Don't question yourself. Take a good look at it. Don't compare it to the imaginary list of others. Remind yourself of the resources, talent, commitment, and passion *you* have at your disposal. Your number one attribute is your attitude. Build it. Use it. You care. You matter!

Leaders are confident.

It's Not Simon Says

When we were little we loved playing the game Simon Says. When it was our turn to be Simon we just loved telling everyone what to do, making sure they did it, and catching them when they made a mistake. That is not leadership. Unfortunately many who are given leadership responsibilities and duties mistake "being bossy" or playing the role of Simon in real life as leadership. No one likes working for or with a 'Simon' so get a better attitude.

There is a big difference between being a boss and a leader.

Take Care of You

Leaders must take care of themselves. Many leaders become workaholics. They really care about their leadership position, the organization, and those they lead. They give and give and sometimes that leads to a detrimental impact on their physical well being. Leaders really need to take care of themselves and sometimes that means putting their health above other commitments. This is a very difficult thing for some to do. They view good leadership as micro management and exhaust themselves and deteriorate their attitude into something their families and coworkers fear rather than respect. Take care of yourself and keep a great attitude.

All of us unfortunately know people that are moody when they are hungry or haven't had enough sleep. Some of us might even be that person. To be a great leader, to acquire that great attitude, we must take care of ourselves physically and mentally. It really matters.

When you eat right, sleep right, and exercise regularly you feel great. When you feel great your attitude improves. I'm talking the basics here. Even brushing your teeth can change your attitude. I cannot emphasize enough how important it is for leaders to take care of themselves. When they don't, their attitude changes, and that adversely effects their ability to lead.

Don't leave rest and nutrition to chance. Know where you are with your health and be proactive about staying in shape. Working out will provide opportunities to reflect. Eating right and getting adequate rest offers practice in discipline. Allow your fitness and health to be a part of your plan to becoming a great leader. Schedule checkups and make time for yourself and family regularly.

Leaders take care of themselves mentally and physically.

Conquer Stress

Stress is a leadership attitude destroyer. Here's how to battle it:

Escape velocity is described as the speed an object needs to be traveling in order break free of a planet's gravitational force. On Earth, escape velocity is seven miles a second, or 25,000 miles an hour. That's fast. The good news is, that once an object reaches escape velocity it no longer requires further propulsion. If the object fails to reach this speed, consequently, it is pulled back. For a long time the science community believed escape velocity was unobtainable. That nothing would ever leave Earth's atmosphere. Now, you and I benefit from the thousands of man-made satellites orbiting our earth. They allow us to communicate, prepare for weather, direct our course and more. Escape velocity achieved. Benefits obtained.

Right now you are sitting with a cold-blooded killer with a similar hold on you.

Stress.

It's real. It's dangerous. It's been identified as the number one killer of all Americans. At times, stress has a gravitational pull on our lives that is seemingly inescapable. Flares of panic. Pangs of anxiety. Stress drives some to madness, addiction, and others, sadly, even worse.

If you are having difficulty escaping your stress you are damaging both mind and body, your relationship, and your employment, but fortunately there is much we can do to obtain the ever-so-needed escape velocity over our stress and move forward with our lives.

The key to our overcoming the consequences of stress, however, is the identical solution of a rocket seeking to escape the planet's strong gravitational pull. Both require an incredible amount of explosive commitment to achieving the result. We are talking sheer brute force and power. We can't try; we must commit. We can't dabble at it. We must go all in. Buckle-up buttercup, it's time for liftoff.

Here are 12 stress-busting tips to help you achieve escape velocity:

1. **Know in your heart and mind that "this too shall pass."** Faith and affirmation are your bodyguards.
2. **Commit to some intense aerobic physical activity.** Workout kids! Get the body moving.
3. **Confide in a close friend or journal.** Get it out of your system. Don't bottle it up.
4. **Prayer.** Best anti-anxiety drug ever made. Find a private place to quiet yourself. Tell the Big Guy what's on your mind. Then listen.
5. **Laugh.** It's time for some 'Three Stooges' or some great comedy. Laughter is awesome medicine.
6. **Face your fear.** Go ahead and describe the worse-case scenario. Look your enemy in the eye. It will instantly shrink before your eyes.
7. **To the war room!** Start developing a plan of attack if your worse fears were to come true. You will find comfort. You'll also find that there is always a solution. When one door closes, another opens.

8. **Fellowship.** Surround yourself with family, activities, and others. You need your tribe. Your tribe needs you.
9. **Get away!** Ever notice your problems shrink as you drive out of town? Put some miles between you and the location of your worry. (You will have to come back. Hawaii is not an option.)
10. **Music.** I have my stress-busting playlist ready. How about you?
11. **Comparison.** You have stress. So does everyone. Pick up a newspaper or go to CNN. Seeing the problems of the world tends to shrink our own. Can't find anyone with a bigger problem? Turn to the obituaries. Oh, and count your blessings.
12. **The size of the hero depends on the size of the problem.** Wanna be a hero? Conquer BIG problems. No one ever got a medal for tying their shoe.

In order to reach escape velocity you'll need to apply all of these with passion and intensity. Doing one of them won't work.

Leaders do not allow stress to negatively influence them.

Build Your Leadership Library

Your attitude is shaped by those you surround yourself with, the books you read, the music you listen to, and the hobbies you keep. Your attitude is strengthened or weakened each day by these and more, and it is up to you to identify what's making you a better leader and what's holding you back. List your strengths. Identify a weakness. Rebuild.

Reading a book will impact your leadership attitude. Reading a book makes you feel better. Again, like exercise you don't need huge swaths of time. A few minutes of day will greatly improve your attitude. Why? Because reading is like taking a mental vacation for a few minutes. You can really escape. Besides reading boosts your intelligence and confidence. Read a few minutes each day and your attitude improves. It's that simple.

I will address reading much more heavily in the chapter on Wisdom, but know nothing changes your attitude more than the books you read.

Leaders collect and build a library of resources to strengthen their attitude.

Use the Comparison Method

The newspaper is one of the most inexpensive and yet most powerful methods for altering your negative attitude. If you are having a bad day go buy a newspaper. Any paper will do. Scan the front page for someone having a day worse than yours.

Your attitude will turn around quickly when you see the problems others must face. Sure, I don't know your past that well, or the difficulties you must face, but I do know the suffering that continues all around this world. Countries where the life expectancy for a male is in the teens. I know places where children walk for miles for water. I know areas where violation and starvation is a regular occurrence. Sure, we have problems, and some are really horrible, but I assure you, not only is someone else suffering worse, somewhere, someone else in history has overcome it. Use comparisons to bust that negative attitude.

Any type of comparison will work. I've read a lot of biographies. In fact I am proud to boast that I have read a biography on every single president of the United States. As an English teacher, I assigned a biography report to all of my students each year. I read a different biography with each class as they read. The result was I read a biography on every president. I read other biographies on some of the most successful people to ever live. They all have one thing in common; each has faced harder challenges than I have. In fact, they not only faced them, they conquered them, and then went on to become successful. It would almost seem that having a challenge in front of you, and a really big one at that, is a prerequisite to success and leadership. The one aspect that each maintained that led them through their difficult time was their attitude. Now I use them as a model for improving my own attitude.

Works of fiction can also be helpful. The bigger the problem in the story, the bigger the hero. No one wants to read about someone whose biggest challenge was crossing a busy street. We immortalize and honor those who overcome big difficulties, not the ones who surrender.

We can also use real people to change our attitude. We have all met someone that has had it worse off than we have. Don't, however, let others lower your standards. You are only permitted to use the comparison method to improve your attitude and improve your leadership.

Leaders keep a good attitude by comparing their problems and challenges to role models that have overcome greater odds.

Whistle While You Work

Your level of self-motivation and passion will directly impact and influence those you lead. Yep! That's your attitude.

How many times have you said, "I can't do that!" or worse, "I don't want to do that!"? There are a lot of unpleasant jobs that need to be done in every area of our life. We have a choice. We can choose to do them with a negative attitude or a positive attitude. It really is that simple. Having a good attitude ensures the job will be done well and the time will move quickly. All will benefit from a good attitude.

I have worked for some leaders that really thought there were certain jobs beneath them to do. They saw themselves as sitting high on a throne ordering others to do the dirty work. I have had other leaders jump right in with me to help get the job done. Guess which one I admired more and had more loyalty? Guess which one I want to follow? It's not the one yelling at me to do it, it's the one working with me to get the job done.

We we can either work for bosses or we work we can work with leaders. We have to do what our boss says, and we want to do what a leader says. Big difference, and it's all in the attitude.

I remember when I was young I had to do a lot of jobs that just seemed absolutely horrible. On one such occasion my father brought home a huge load of wood that needed to be sawed and split for our wood-burning stove. The pile of wood looked like a mountain. There was no way I could do it alone. My dad explained to me how the job would build character and muscle. He told me how we could save money heating the house with the wood. Nothing he said, however, changed my attitude. This job was beneath me, in my mind, and something that I wanted no part of at all.

All of my friends that weekend were watching the big ball game and here I was stuck behind the house on a freezing-cold day cutting and sorting wood. I had the worst attitude in the world. My dad had other work to do and I was left alone.

Lucky for me my brother surprised us with a visit home. He found me in the back yard mumbling about the work I had to do. I was doing it slowly and poorly. In just a few seconds my brother had turned the entire chore into a fun game. He had a wonderful knack for doing that. He was a true leader. We put the ball game on the radio and made a contest out of the work. I remember my brother making up this silly song parody on "The Devil Came Down to Georgia" about our job. In my brother's version it was our hometown, not Georgia and the contest wasn't fiddling, it was…splitting wood. I laughed so hard my side hurt. The job was completed in no time at all, I enjoyed it, and I did a good job. Dad was happy. I learned a valuable lesson that day.

What seemed like an agonizing job ended up being one of the most memorable weekends with my brother. We traded stories, laughed, and had a good time. I learned a lot about leadership that weekend. Many hands really do lighten the load, and a good attitude makes the work go by faster. You really do better work with a great attitude too.

My brother did not have to help me, but by doing so he showed me the importance of the job and how to do it right. My brother still leads that way, and so do I. As the general manager of a prominent hotel he had over twenty managers to do any job that needed done, but time after time, I have witnessed my brother leading from the front and doing even the most menial job himself. He always has a great attitude and that sets the tone for everyone that works for him.

My dad was right too. All winter long when we heated that house I felt proud of cutting all the wood. My dad usually complained about the bills in the house, but that winter every time a heating bill arrived he sang my praises to everyone in the family about how my hard work saved the family money. It was one of the first times I really felt like a man in our family.

Leaders know doing a job well is only half of the job; leaders do it with a great attitude.

Respond. Don't React.

In short, don't lose your cool. Having a positive attitude means you don't lose your temper. You don't want to be the type of leader that reacts to situations, but rather one that responds. Problems are going to happen. That's why we need leaders. Call it job security and expect them to arrive.

Leaders are the ones who not only know what to do when a problem arises, but likes doing it. When problems occur, a leader responds in a way that produces options, and ultimately, a solution. Exploding in anger only makes the problem worse. This is true for a leader of a major corporation, the leader of a family, and leaders at any level. Keep your attitude in check and create options.

If the people you are leading fear your reaction, they are not going to report a problem, and if they do, it will most likely be in an untimely manner. You want to demonstrate how a problem should be handled to those you lead. If you react with anger and contempt that is what you are teaching everyone in your organization. If you react with contemplation and options, so will those you lead.

All of the praise, acknowledgements and reinforcements you have put into place to boost morale and work ethics can be annihilated with one bout of *losing your cool*. It always takes twenty positive comments to replace one negative comment said in anger.

Confidence offers the leader much, but probably nothing greater than the ability to respond rather than react. Always take the time to formulate a response rather than fire off a reaction. Responses are given after a period of reflection and leave little doubt to how they will be received. The leader has measured and calculated the response and impact well. Reactions are at best, gut-responses that are fired off in some emotive state. How a reaction will be received is anyone's guess. Stay clear of reacting and focus on responding. Reflect then respond.

Leaders quickly formulate a response and steer clear of reacting.

When something goes wrong how do you respond?

Are you first to identify it? That's good. We need people that can identify areas for improvement, but something still needs to be done about it.

Are you first to vocalize a complaint about it? That could be good, because others could suffer or be harmed by a fault that hasn't been identified, but again, something has to be done. Did your vocalized observation put some solution into action?

Are you first to fix it? That's great! We really need problem solvers in the world. There are a lot of people quick to identify problems, but so few to act.

People pride themselves on delegating problems onto others. I think that can be very useful at times, but more often than not, there are just so many little things we can all do that would make the world easier for each other. We are so quick to evaluate problems of all different sizes as *not our problem*. That piece of paper in the hallway, *not mine*. The snack machine isn't working, well, *someone else will report it*. And so on.

We spend our day with our list of to-dos, and job descriptions, but we fail to realize there really is a whole world of problems that aren't on anyone's list. They grow, multiply, and eventually hurt people.

Every now and then we spot someone special that seems to go out of his or her way, to fix a problem that clearly isn't *their problem*. And we think, "Wow! I'd like to be like them." And we either do, or don't emulate their actions. In reality, we would find that they didn't really go out of their way much at all. In fact, they not only made their day easier by fixing that problem, but ours as well.

So, go ahead, and be first to fix it. See what happens.

•••

Do you remember hearing about the JetBlue Flight Attendant, Steven Slater, who was **having a bad day**? He decided to cuss-out the passengers he was supposed to be caring for, aboard JetBlue Flight 10512 over the public address system. He then grabbed some beers, deployed the emergency slide, and fled to his nearby home where he was arrested. Now, before I sound-off on Steven Slater, and I will, let me assure you I laughed heartily, and I truly couldn't get enough of this modern day spin of **Take this Job and Shove It,** when the news first broke. What an odd and hilarious story!

And then reality set in.

Despite how the media portrays what happened, Steven Slater is no folk hero, and his actions are anything but admirable. Sure, all of us at times get frustrated with coworkers, customers, bosses, and our jobs, but Slater's actions are troubling. It makes a great headline and some incredible conversation, but nothing more.

Admittedly, I do not know all of the events, but I feel very safe saying he went overboard. Way overboard! We all have moments that could certainly make the beginnings of a bad day, but it's only when we surrender to that moment does our day go south and end up sour.

What should we do to prevent a bad day? Here's my advice:

1. **Give up some gratitude!** When you feel the pressure building to a point that you aren't sure you can handle it, start thinking of people, situations and things in your life for which you are thankful. When you start thinking about what you are thankful for it puts your life in perspective. You remember it's not just you. Others are counting on you. And the biggie... many, many people have it worse than you and would trade spots with you in an instant.

2. **Hit the restart button**. There is no reset button, because you can never erase the score or hit the reset button like you can in a video game. You can't turn back the clock in life, nor would you really want to. (You'd never get anywhere.) But you can hit the restart button and give it another try. Your bruises don't magically go away, and you may have to apologize, but you can restart your day at any time regardless of how bad it gets.

3. **Do the next right thing**. You do not have to be perfect. In fact, you can't. No need trying. Just try to do the next right thing. Just one right thing at a time. Live in the now and make it count.

4. **Find the funny.** There is something funny in every situation. Try to find it. Have a laugh. Point out the ridiculous and the absurd, then get back at it.

5. **Call a time out.** Find a co-worker, your boss, anybody, and tell them that you need a minute or two to collect yourself. Do whatever you need to do to get away from the situation and take

a super-short break.

We have a responsibility to others, a responsibility to contribute to society and we are accountable for all that we do, as well as what we don't do.

Keep Some Rose Colored Glasses Nearby

One of my friends asked me why I was always so positive. The answer is simple and it's a very large part of my secret to what success I have achieved. I see the world in a very unique way. I view every person I meet, every person I contact, and anyone I encounter as if they are the brightest, kindest, most helpful person I have ever met. Furthermore, I truly believe it. I believe that the people I meet absolutely want to help me succeed and that they are waiting for the opportunity to work with me. You know what? It almost always works out as I picture it too.

Have you heard about the Pygmalion Effect? It comes from George Bernard Shaw's story *Pygmalion*, better known probably to most as the movie My Fair Lady. The Pygmalion Effect has been incorporated into school settings with teachers and students. When teachers *believe* they have received the best students, whether they actually have or not, or when students believe they have received the finest teachers, they respond accordingly and excel. Even when it's not true. The attitude of positive assumption tilts the favor in their odds.

I don't apply this Pygmalion Effect for sheer personal gain. I have always believed people should be measured on their best day, not their worst, and I know from personal experience that most people rise to the expectations to which they are held. So why not hold everyone to a high expectation? Also, it fits with the Golden Rule; I would want people to expect the same from me on our first meeting.

Those who have low opinions of others or go in to a meeting with preconceived negative thoughts are unaware that those very negative thoughts often reveal themselves in the person's eyes, tone, and body language. People can recognize if you think less of them. Other people pick up how you view people. It is an unspoken attitude that tells others about you long before you say a single word.

Leaders look for the best in others and most often find it.

Spend time with those who celebrate you, not tolerate you.

Begin with Gratitude

I once read a powerful quote that went something like, "If you can't be thankful for what you have, be thankful for what you have avoided." I just love the power of quotes. In order to have a great attitude as a leader you must be gracious. There is always something to be thankful for in any situation regardless of how bleak it seems. Be thankful for all that you have and begin your day by giving thanks. Run through your mind all to which you can offer thanks. Be thankful for the material things you have, the people in your life, your mental health, your physical health, opportunities, your faith, a good attitude, and anything else that crosses your mind. Get your journal out and brainstorm your thanks if necessary. Giving gratitude puts your entire day in perspective. Your problems begin to shrink. When you look for the best, you find it. You're not avoiding the problems; you're focusing on the goal.

So many wise and helpful leaders have shared with me the importance of gratitude. Each emphasized the need to begin our day being grateful, and in times of doubt or trouble reminding ourselves of our blessings. It works. Every time I have encountered some dismal prospect, I remind myself of the great opportunities and people I have been surrounded with in my lifetime. My attitude instantly gets back on track.

Leaders have an attitude of gratitude.

Everyone can lead! One of the most important lessons anyone can ever learn about leadership is that you can lead without a title or a position of authority. You don't need to be the president, captain, or chairperson. Many times I have seen the person designated as captain shrink under pressure, and witnessed *an unknown* rise and fill the absent leadership role. The latter truly had the attitude of a leader, and the former had the title.

Ask yourself, "If not me, then who?" It isn't very often that you will get a phone call or letter requesting you to lead. Most leaders aren't elected either. The vast majority of leaders are hewn from answering a single question: If not me, then who? The attitude of a leader can be summed up with the internal willingness to want to make a difference in the world. That's the key ingredient. Leaders have a desire to make a difference, not hold a position of authority.

When you lead without a title people see it and recognize it. The next time there is a need to fill a leadership role or position, your actions will be remembered. You'll be nominated, you'll get the vote, or the promotion.

Leadership must happen before the title is given or the votes counted. Leadership isn't a title.

Loosen up

A leader should be fun to work with. You never work *for* a leader. You work *with* leaders. You work for bosses. A leader's attitude shouldn't be entirely authoritative. A leader creates an environment where people are excited about showing up and getting results.

I mentioned that leaders need confidence and a little swagger in their walk, but when they take everything way too seriously they become a type of person no one wants to be around let alone follow or work alongside. Learn to laugh and have some fun. Leadership is about people and influencing lives.

Leaders don't get caught up in being leaders, they focus on working with people and making a difference.

Attitude is a choice. When you are able to fully apply this truth you will be in charge of your attitude and people will be attracted to you, people will listen to you, and you will be able to help accomplish great things. I cannot stress this principle more clearly, nor highlight its truth; attitude is a choice.

Take an interest in others. Have an attitude of sincere interest. Ask questions. Get to know the people you work alongside and lead.

> *"Effective leaders attempt to understand the people they lead."*
> **~Christopher Layton**

Know that you were put here to do something great and make a contribution to the lives of others.

You must understand that you are responsible for those you lead and the decisions that you make. You must understand that your decisions will impact lives. Make sure the impact is always for the better.

An Attitude of Commitment

The bottom line is simple: Great leaders have great attitudes. Effective leaders are always working on and improving their attitude. They are consistently making small tweaks and adjustments in how they deal with others as well as guard the thinking that goes on in their mind. Great leaders are very careful about what thoughts they allow to persist in their minds.

The other five essentials in this book will do much to strengthen you attitude. They complement and nurture one another. When you lift weights, the wrist strengthens as the bicep grows because one impacts the other. The forearm also strengthens, as does the shoulder! You cannot help but strengthen the surrounding muscles while focusing on one, because they compliment each other. The same is true when working on becoming a better leader. Work on one essential quality and you gradually build the others too. So, when building: communication skills, wisdom, authenticity, tenacity, or your leadership vision, you will be improving your attitude.

Commitment 1

The First Leadership Commitment
I will lead with a great attitude.

I fully understand that my attitude is under my complete control. I understand the important correlation between leading and having a good, personal attitude. I will work daily on improving my attitude and the attitudes of those I lead.

CHAPTER 5

Wisdom

There is a difference between intelligence and wisdom. Possessing both are ideal, but the latter is the king of leadership. Wisdom is a journey.

You hear the word wisdom and I'll bet many of you picture an old guy with a long white beard on the side of a mountain. Quit it.

Wisdom can be most easily defined as the ability to consistently make good decisions. While this is a very simple definition, the process requires all of your talents, experiences, and resources to be put into action.

Leaders certainly want to make good decisions. As a leader we must fully understand that our decisions can impact the life of others. Our role of leader implies an unspoken responsibility for the care and well being of others through the decisions we make. Your decisions should embody forethought, empathy, and fairness. Therefore, a better definition for **wisdom**, I believe, is: **the ability to see the future consequences of the decisions you make right now.**

Wisdom is wholeheartedly about *your* personal development. Many people look at their calendar, their to-do list, and all of the responsibilities they have taken on and decide that they have no more time for further personal development. I tell you, there is no man or woman despite their success and responsibilities, that can afford to remain unattended to their personal development for more than a day.

A leader needs to understand that the decisions he makes has future consequences and impacts the lives of many. Great care and consideration must be weighed before making decisions. Wisdom will allow the leader to make great decisions.

So where does wisdom come from? I mentioned it is a combination of our experiences, talents, and resources, so we will need to examine each. But you must know that wisdom is a journey, not a destination. A great leader is always pursuing wisdom, and the sad truth is that its attainment is never truly attainable, but that is also the essence of its brilliance. You might eventually be described as wise, but you are only truly wise if you are still on the journey seeking wisdom.

If you are constantly on the journey toward wisdom and filling yourself of its fruits along the way, never knowing how close you are to the prize, you will never stop developing this essential leadership skill. Wisdom is recognizing your need to know more and constantly seeking it.

Seek wisdom. Wisdom will not be delivered to you. You must go find wisdom. Most people, don't even bother looking. Most people become satisfied with what they know and what they are doing. The wise are constantly asking questions, reading, and seeking new experiences.

Unsuccessful leaders assume they are wise because they have obtained some leadership title or role. They believe they have been doing something so long, they must be good at it and are therefore wise. Others confuse wisdom with age. This unfortunately is too common and incorrect. There are many, who over time do in fact acquire a great deal of wisdom, but just because someone is young does not mean they aren't capable of obtaining wisdom and being wise. Just because someone is old or has been doing something a long time, doesn't necessarily make their ideas best or worthy of being followed.

Wisdom is an admission that you have a lot to learn and it's also a pledge that you will go and seek it. Wisdom is therefore not the having of knowledge, but the constant journey toward searching for answers.

"By three methods we may learn wisdom: First, by reflection, which is noblest; Second, by imitation, which is easiest; and third by experience, which is the bitterest."
-Confucius

So what's the difference between intelligence and wisdom? Much. Intelligence is just one small part of wisdom. Intelligence serves you right now. Wisdom serves others long after you are gone. You can have intelligence and yet lack wisdom. I have witnessed many intelligent people who have made poor choices. They made a bad decision because they based their choice only on their intelligence. There are many factors that make up wisdom, and intelligence is only one of its many spokes. I believe receiving an education, and earning a degree, or even multiple degrees is wonderful, but not for the sake of having titles. A wise person is well rounded. Those who truly possess wisdom have taken chances, received an education, worked hard jobs, read books, had great conversations with diverse groups of people, traveled, and noticed the nature around them. Wise people observe, listen, investigate, and contribute.

Wisdom is a journey. A big part of wisdom is discovering what you don't know, and allowing others to fill in the gaps and pick up the slack. Wisdom doesn't mean you know everything. The reality of wisdom is understanding you don't know everything, can't be expected to know everything, and that you certainly aren't going to pretend you do. Wisdom is the willingness to learn, weigh the advice and counsel of others, and ask big questions. Wisdom is a journey we must accept to take in order to become a leader.

The first step on the journey to wisdom is recognizing the need for wisdom in your life. Just the mere decision to seek wisdom, instantly makes you wiser. Truly. Having this awareness and internal drive to become wiser will start the journey and bring you closer to wisdom and becoming a better leader. You will evaluate the decisions of others with greater scrutiny, you will weigh the words in the books you read with greater influence, and you will begin to seek the best solutions for the problems you face.

So where do we begin in our quest for wisdom? Well, it certainly starts with education, but that is far too limiting. I have met plenty of well educated people that I would certainly not consider wise, and even more whose schooling was limited, but have built a dynasty of wise decisions. An education serves us best when it ignites a fire within us to become lifelong learners. **Wisdom is the sum of the intelligence you gain educating yourself, the experiences of traveling, the life experiences and insight from friends, as well as the discipline and awareness gained from private reflection.**

Have you ever noticed that successful leaders seem to do many things well? It is by no accident that this occurs. Successful leaders are committed to excellence and a desire to be at the top of their game and make an impact in the world. They hold themselves to a higher standard than anyone else does. They seek self improvement. **This drive to make a difference in their lives and in the lives of others is the foundation of wisdom.**

The measure of wisdom can be determined by four factors: 1) The books you read. 2) The people with whom you surround yourself. 3) The time you spend in contemplation. 4) Your combined experiences.

1) **Read great books.** Read books that will change your life. The average American reads just one book a year. How sad! Challenge yourself to read one a month. Read a book on leadership, finances, parenting, a biography, or anything that interests you. Reading a good book is like living another life. Books are the building blocks of wisdom.

Albert Einstein is quoted as saying, "Know where to find the information and how to use it; that's the secret of success." That's great advice and another key on our journey to wisdom. My dad always told me, "If you don't know the answer, at least know where you can find it." As a result, our home was filled with lots and lots of books. I think one of the greatest gifts my parents gave me was this desire to learn, especially through books. Always keep a good book near you.

You should read twelve books a year!

For some, twelve books a year seems like a Herculean task. If you break it down, it's obviously one book a month, but how do we tackle that? For still some, one book a month seems too much. My suggestion is read for just ten minutes a day. That's your goal. Believe it or not, but ten minutes each and every day will add up to give you five hours of reading each month. I think for most that would be enough time to finish a book. Those ten minutes a day will really serve you well when spent in a book and will encourage you along your path to wisdom.

What twelve books should I read? Well, it would be great if a couple of those were my books, but what I want to stress is that the twelve you read impact and help shape your life. Here are some areas you should try to include:

1. Read a book about relationships.
2. Read a book about finances.
3. Read a book about parenting.
4. Read a book about healthier living.
5. A "classic work" of literature by one of the greats.
6. Read a book on your favorite hobby.
7. Read a book about your faith.
8. Read a self-help book.
9. Read a best seller.
10. Read a book on your career.
11. Read a biography on a person in history you admire.
12. Read a cookbook or any how-to book.

Even if you don't make your goal of twelve, you will gain so much for having tried. As Les Brown says, "Shoot for the moon and even if you miss you will be among the stars." You will live the life you plan. Just imagine yourself the year after reading this list of books; you would be a better partner, friend, employee, entrepreneur, parent, brother, athlete, have better health, and so much more. Read books on the lives of those who have led and learn from both their mistakes and their accomplishments.

If you would like a list of the books that I believe will impact your life please send me an email at info@kellycroy.com and ask me for The Book List. I will be happy to send it to you. These are of course the books that influenced me. In truth, however, any books read will add to your wisdom.

Leading and learning go hand in hand. A good leader always understands that she must learn more. A bad or ineffective leader is one that believes either she knows everything, or that she knows more than everyone else.

2) **Keep company with quality people.** Surround yourself with people who you admire, hold you to a higher standard, challenge you to become a better person, and that are steadfast in morality and ideals. You can learn more about leadership by being in the company of leaders you respect and admire, than a library of books. Spend time with these leaders. Volunteer to help them if needed, but find a way to meet, talk, and spend time with them. Don't set your standards low either. Social media has provided us with the opportunity to ask questions and 'virtually' talk with leaders that ordinarily we would never get to meet.

Surround Yourself With Quality: I love the old saying, "Lie down with dogs, and wake up with fleas." Its value has become more and more apparent with each year of my life, especially with those I have taught, mentored, and coached. For some reason, human nature I suppose, most people prefer to learn this lesson on their own.

A leader truly shows wisdom by surrounding himself with great people. You need to surround yourself with people who help you form decisions, provide positive life-lessons and serve as role models. My friend Andy Andrews, an international speaker, author, and humorist, came up with a great idea. Andy created a board of directors that he bounces ideas off. He chose the best people he knew from all walks of life and uses them for every decision. The real beauty of Andy's idea, and what makes it hilarious, is that none of them know they're on his board. I love it and use it! (Never be afraid to use a good idea just because it isn't yours; just be sure to give credit where credit is due.) He just imagines what these "board members" would think of his decision and acts accordingly. Brilliant idea Andy! That's why Andy is on my "board" too.

Surround yourself with advisors and teammates that can help you find the answer. You need a group of diverse people. Sure, there needs to be a common thread of integrity and passion, but having a diverse group of unique individuals to bounce ideas off is important. You need creatives, visionaries, realists, dreamers, left-brained, right-brained, and whatever else you can find. Even if they are not at your immediate disposal, create a relationship with these talents for future collaborations.

3) **Spend time each day in introspection.** This can be accomplished through journaling, contemplation, meditation, silence, or prayer. (Not napping.) This can be a time for formulating the questions that guide us, or a quiet time to work on a virtue. Start by giving gratitude for all that you have, then tighten your focus on positive questions that will guide you where you want to go. Don't use this time to worry or think negatively. Your reflection time should be void of emotion. It's a time to weigh all sides. How much time should you invest? Well, that is up to the individual, but ten minutes a day would be a solid start.

Four Powerful Yet Unlikely Introspection Techniques Used by Olympic Athletes

A. Visualization: Visualizing a situation in a positive way helps you prepare. Your mind doesn't know the difference. I know, this sounds a little farfetched, however, tests on Olympic athletes have demonstrated the mind cannot differentiate between an actual occurrence and an imagined one. We can prepare ourselves for situations by imagining positive outcomes. Positive visualization prepares us for success and overcoming challenges. Negative visualization steers our subconscious toward making poor choices and ultimately failure.

How to employ visualization: We get better at what we practice. The same is true for visualization, meditation, and affirmation. We need practice. Visualization is the opposite of meditation. When we visualize we want as many details involved in the mind as possible. Try to include all of the senses. All of them. Repeat daily. Try to think of the sounds, smells, and imagery of the environment and the process of what a successful resolution would include.

Whether I am competing in a triathlon or giving a new art presentation, I imagine myself doing it well, repeatedly. I see myself smiling. I feel the coolness of the water, the uncomfortable seat, the rigorous run. I imagine obstacles and myself successfully overcoming them. I see the time on my watch, just a little better than my last swim, run, or bike. Always a little improvement, but within the realm of possibility. If my mind works against me and inserts a failure I just rewind my imaginary mental video and replay it until it is the way I want it. It works! My visualizations last only a few minutes. Sometimes I even perform research to learn about the new location I will be traveling to or people I will meet. I arrive with confidence. Our minds are powerful. Use visualization.

How does visualization make us wiser? If our brain doesn't know the difference between what actually happens and what we visualize, we gain wisdom through each added experience as if it were practice. And this is exactly what Olympic athletes do. This is how they train. They visualize themselves throwing farther, shaving a millisecond off their time, getting an extra rep, winning the gold. They are taught to make their visualizations as real as possible. They utilize all of their senses. And… it works.

B. Reflection: When we take time to reflect upon what we have learned and accomplished we become wise. Periods of reflection can be achieved in many ways, including: reteaching, discussing, journaling, and video or audio diary entries, to name but a few.

The idea of reflecting is simply reserving a short period of time to think about and record what you have learned and figure out where you need to go.

Reflecting is about measuring, comparing, evaluating, questioning, and reviewing what you've done, what you haven't done, what you need to stop doing, and what needs to be accomplished.

Reflecting is a process that *first gathers all the positives* and then the negatives. It is important that we review our gains and earnings first. Always figure out what you did *right* before you begin correcting yourself or anyone else.

The journal has served as my reflection tool of choice simply because I can travel back in time through the pages and see how I overcame obstacles in the past. Journal reflection has served me well, and I highly recommend it to you as well.

There is a growing trend of people using social media tools for personal reflection and goal setting. I am sure this can work well, though I am personally careful about what I wish to share and you should be too. Reflection should at first be private. Later, you can decide what questions to share to further your wisdom.

C. Meditation: For many, the word meditation brings forth religious or cult-like images. That is certainly not the meditation I am referring to here. Meditation is merely a slowing down from the hustle and bustle of life's many demanding tasks and busyness, and allowing ourselves time to relax our brain. Meditation is quite simply a time to discipline the mind, slow down, and provide ourselves with an opportunity to enrich our lives with a type of wisdom known to leaders throughout history, but also one that escapes so many in this age of multi-tasking.

Ever wonder why you get such great ideas while you are in the shower or in the bathroom? Curious why your brain gets flooded with thoughts and ideas right at bedtime? Is commuting to work one of your most creative environments? It very well may be the first time you have allowed your physical self and mental self to catch up with one another, and offered yourself the gift of reflection. Your brain is sorting through and addressing what it feels is important.

The reason we get such great ideas in the shower is simple. Your eyes are closed. You are in a confined space. For the most part you are still. The heat and feel of the water, or a confined environment create an environment perfect for reflecting. Without knowing it, you have created a perfect meditation chamber. For similar reasons, that is why we get ideas in our cars and other places that force us to stop and bring the mind and body together for a short period of time.

Meditation is simply a built-in period of time to reflect and slow down. Sherlock Holmes enjoyed staring out a window with his violin, Stephen King and Steve Jobs enjoyed walking to think and reflect. Bill Gates prefers to rock in a chair. Others enjoy sitting in a chair or on the floor. Meditation is a reserved time to stop your physical self and control your mind. It isn't as simple as you think. It takes some practice and discipline but it will advance you on your path toward wisdom.

How to meditate

I recommend finding a room free of people where you can shut the door. Sit in a chair with great posture. You don't want to be too comfortable. Place your hands on your thighs. Plug your feet into the floor. Take ten slow and deep breaths with your eyes closed. Inhale through your nose and exhale through your mouth. Think of nothing. Push thoughts away. We want a totally blank canvas. When something enters the canvas, and it will, simply remove it and return it to emptiness. Repeat. When the urge to itch your nose, ear, chin or shuffle your feet arises, and it will, ignore it. Your goal is to remain like this for five to ten minutes. You will fail many times. It's like going to the weight room. The more times you do it the easier it is, and the greater your results. Build a strong mind. Build discipline.

Wisdom is gained through reflection. While the period of meditation itself is not quite reflection, it disciplines the mind to better handle moments of reflection and decision. It also reduces stress, which is the enemy of all leaders.

D. Affirmations and negative self talk: I once read that 95 percent of the average person's words they say to themselves are negative. "I can't do that!" or "That was horrible," "I should just quit," and "I'll never get this right." Just to name a few.

This negative self talk is counter productive to leaders and anyone working toward success. Replace you negative words to yourself with positive affirmations.

Rather than saying, "That was horrible!" replace it with, "I will improve on that!" or "Practice makes perfect so I better try that again."

Remember that what you say to yourself truly matters. We become what we describe ourselves as and we need our self talk to be positive and nurturing. Everything we say and everything we do, matters!

Catch yourself talking negatively or berating yourself, and stop it!

Immediately talk to yourself out loud what you should have said. I know that sounds silly, but in time you will have corrected this harmful habit. This also works if you have a problem with profanity.

Add Affirmations! Add some affirmations to your daily self talk. Since we have already established that everyone talks to themselves, and that the majority of our self talk is negative, it would be a good plan to purposely say some positive and helpful words of encouragement throughout our day. What could we say to ourselves that would be better than the negative statements we are making? What would help us look at a setback differently? What words will improve our outcome and our attitude?

An affirmation is a positive statement we say to ourselves to create a desired purpose or effect. Affirmations help us to change our attitudes and our outcomes. Affirmations are powerful. You must create some powerful affirmations and employ them daily.

What affirmations will we create? We might first want to identify some of the negative self talk we are already using and replace it with a positive affirmation. This would be easy to reword, but if we are not fully aware of our negative self talk we can still create some affirmations to use.

Some Example Affirmations:
1. Wow! That was a bad choice! I am going to turn this around. Lesson learned.
2. Well, that's the last time I'll do that.
3. Yes! Practice makes perfect.
4. Every day I'm getting healthier and wealthier! Keep making good choices!

You can think of situations where you know you will need some positive self talk, or incidents where you have failed in the past. Perhaps you need some affirmation the next time someone cuts in front of you in traffic, or you forget something at home. Get creative! Affirmations really help. We become what we talk about.

4) **Continuously add new experiences to your life.** Travel. Meet new people. Take on new challenges. Serve others. The greatest opportunities for wisdom are those where you can work alongside others, especially when those you work with have diverse and unique experiences. Take on new roles and positions. Volunteer for something new. Eat lunch with someone different each day. Consistently seek opportunities to collaborate with others whose work you admire.

I am convinced that new experiences are one of the best ways to further your journey on the path toward wisdom. Make time to get away from the closed environment you work and live in and add to your routine experiences. Wisdom can be found by stepping out of your comfort zone and trying something new.

Conferences are great for everyone, not just professionals. If you want to be a better parent, travel and talk with parents who are doing amazing things with their children. If you are a student, visit another school. The goal here is to go somewhere new and experience life from a new point of view.

Reading, keeping the company of admirable people, reflecting, and traveling are incredibly powerful to gaining wisdom when applied with the right attitude. Each will serve you well on your journey to becoming a successful leader.

The journey toward wisdom is an essential quality of leadership, and a big part of acquiring wisdom is surrounding yourself with quality people each and every day. Some of you may have a choice in who will be part of your team or inner circle, so make your decisions carefully. Others will not have a choice of whom they will work closely with and lead. Regardless, wisdom is gained by not only making good choices, but nurturing everyone you work with into becoming world-class leaders. Grow the realm of your wisdom and invest in cultivating leadership. Create a leadership factory within your organization and produce leaders.

Help others become leaders by giving them leadership roles or responsibilities. Let them know they are leading and give them a framework to work within. Tell them, "You will be leading our organization on this area. I know you can do it. I want to give you plenty of freedom on this, but I do need a report or update on where you are at the close of each day and we certainly want to have this project complete by this date." I know so many micromanagers that need to control too much of the organization that they never give anyone the opportunity to lead, to fail, to grow. Then they wonder why they have no leadership. You have to grow leaders and nurture them.

Offer those around you mentors to help them become better leaders, and by all means be an excellent and available role model yourself. Surround them with books, audio, video, and other resources to help them become leaders. Make all of these resources easily available. Send them to conferences, invite speakers, leave them notes of encouragement and helpful tips to follow. I have spoken at many workshops and provided leadership training and the comments are always the same, "I wish we would have done this sooner." Leadership is something you have to manufacture. Start your leadership factory today.

Invite those you lead to reflect on leadership by writing an article for the newsletter or blog. Consider asking the promising leader to organize and lead a presentation on something they are doing well. Ask their opinion about leadership topics and books they are reading on leadership. Engaging in this dialogue will reinforce the qualities you desire and want perpetuated.

By all means, recognize those who lead. This will encourage everyone. Make leadership important and something that is identified and recognized. When recognition is implemented correctly it can increase retention, decrease absence, raise production, improve quality, change attitudes, and in general create a momentum of success and positive energy.

What ideas do you have about building a leadership factory within your organization? How will you prepare, train, equip, and acknowledge leaders? How will you design and build your leadership factory? By all means, recognize those who lead. This will encourage everyone.

How to recognize leaders within your organization: It has been wisely stated that a great leader humbly accepts the failures of his organization as his own, and passes any praise and success on as the accomplishments of his colleagues. In addition, I have always been reminded that a great leader criticizes in private and praises in public. Clearly, recognition is an essential act of leadership. Clearly recognition is important, but so many organizations get it wrong. Many in leadership positions just don't know how to effectively implement a recognition program, acknowledge someone for their efforts, or how to reward employees.

It's all about making it personal.

Leaders have a responsibility to recognize the accomplishments of those within their organization. It is one of the most important duties of a leader. When it is handled well, it really is beautiful and people talk about it for a long time. When it is handled poorly, it is ugly, and people talk about that for a long time too. More important is the impact both have on the people that make the magic happen within your organization.

How to make recognition work!

Recognition is powerful. I believe, however, very few organizations get this right. While it is never a bad time to recognize the good works of others, there are some ideas to consider:

- **Let people know exactly what you want**. If they know what you want they can work toward the goal. Don't leave people guessing. Be direct. *These are the results we reward.*
- **Recognition should be meaningful.** Everyone knows when someone deserves the recognition. Don't reward people because *it's their turn.* That's a step backward. Don't be afraid to recognize individuals. Sure teams need recognition, but individual recognition is the most powerful form possible.
- **Great recognition is most often inexpensive or free.** Everyone wants to hear praise. Write them a note. Send them a gift card. Tell others *the story* of why they were recognized.
- **Recognition shouldn't be predictable.** Mix it up. Keep everyone guessing and surprised.
- **Great recognition is memorable.** When you tell their story, mention them by name, and make them feel deserving; they'll remember it. You don't need to send them to Hawaii. Unless of course, you can.
- **Don't be afraid to reward the same person more than once, or in a row.** Make it personal. You're not just rewarding people, you're rewarding the action you want replicated.
- **Encourage others to create their own recognition programs and awards.** Let others partake in meaningful recognition. Encourage it. Support it. Participate.

One of my favorite speaking engagements is when I am asked to share my art and words at an award's banquet or recognition dinner. I love participating in the recognition of others and retelling an amazing story of achievement. I can see it in the eyes of the recipient when I shake their hand and present them with a piece of customized art. They didn't even know how awesome they were because they were just doing their best and giving their all. Now someone is telling an amazing story of accomplishment, and it's about them! You can also tell that they will pay forward whatever recognition they received, ten fold. They will continue with even greater tenacity to innovate and make a difference. *They* matter… therefore *recognition* matters.

How will you create your leadership factory?

Master the core base of knowledge of your organization!

To lead you must know what you are talking about. In fact, you need to know each job within your organization well. You must be able to explain the job of every individual you lead. You are not expected to perform the job as well as each individual, but you need to understand its core purpose and expectations. The quarterback on the football team needs to know where each player is when a play is called, and so do you.

You also must understand the central purpose of your organization, the role each individual plays, and how each can continually add value to it. If you are able to do this, you are on the road to wisdom and on the road to becoming a good leader. If not, this is where you must begin.

You must commit your profession's core base of knowledge to absolute mastery. Coaches must know their plays, teachers must know their lessons, and doctors must know their anatomy. Each person must continue adding to the core, perhaps by conducting research and working to further their knowledge and experience, but a core level of mastery must be achieved for competency and confidence. You can always learn more about what you are doing.

Too often I have been called to consult with a corporation about engaging leaders within the work place only to find many of the leaders and managers don't even know what some of their employees do during the day. What a startling revelation! Know your people like family and know their job like your own. How can you possibly motivate or inspire someone you don't know? How can you lead or manage a position you don't fully understand? Don't be afraid to ask questions of those you lead. They will feel valued and you will elevate the importance of their position. And… you will learn. Don't pretend to know what you truly don't.

Ask yourself, "What do I need to know?"

Wisdom is about the questions you ask.

When you don't know something, admit it. Wisdom is about understanding what you don't know, discovering those weaknesses, and fortifying them. Only a fool would hide a weakness and hope it remains under cover.

We must ask questions. The better questions we ask, the wiser we become.

Leaders ask questions. Outstanding leaders ask outstanding questions.

Who wants to know?

Sometimes we become frustrated when someone asks us a question. Sometimes we become frustrated when we don't know the answer to something. We think to ourselves that answering is a step backward. To the contrary, answering questions, is a form of teaching, and helps us to master our content.

We become less frustrated when the person asking us a question is someone we admire and respect. We need to listen to what questions we ask ourselves. In our mind, we need to imagine someone else doing the asking. A great way to listen to the question is to **reconsider the question** as if it is being asked by someone else, someone you respect and admire. Take the same question and ask it again imagining someone you respect asking it. It really changes the question doesn't it? The question now helps you look at the situation differently. The question improves you.

What would a parent want to know?

What would your customer want to know?

What would a new teammate want to know?

What would Steve Jobs want to know?

Taking the power of questions to a new level, I recommend creating a Frequently Asked Questions (FAQ) page for yourself in your leadership role. Create a list as a reminder of great questions to ask yourself from time to time, when you encounter a problem, or admire a success. Use this list and add to it as a refresher or reference.

Here is a powerful list of questions. Feel free to add to this list:

- What is good about this problem?
- What can I do to make this situation fun?
- What do I need to keep doing?
- What do I need to stop doing?
- What do I need to start doing?
- Does this support my core values?
- Who does this help? Who does this hurt?
- What will this cost in both time and finances?
- Is it time for this?
- Even though we **can** do this, should we?
- How will those I admire and love respect my decision?
- Does this further us along on our goals and vision or hold us back?
- What will this mean to me and those I love if I am successful?
- What will it mean to me and those I love if I never even start?

A leader is made from the questions she asks herself. These questions serve as a great start to some personal reflection and introspection.

Wisdom from minimizing.

One of the greatest experiences of my life was working as a program aide during college summers at the reknown Perkins School for the Blind in Watertown, Massachusetts. This remarkable experience steeled me for a career in teaching and even prepared me for fatherhood. I learned much about patience, serving others, and how to never, ever lose my keys.

My job at Perkins was basically to assist with the needs of five blind, autistic students, and help out with their extracurricular activities and outings. I helped them get to class, assisted them with their meals and care, and I made certain they had fun. We spent a lot of time together in and out of the cottage. Perkins was my home during several New England summers.

Until I arrived at Perkins I had never been around a blind person. I was studying to be an educator, and I had hoped to hone my teaching skills with the boys in my cottage, however it was they who really taught me. The lessons in patience and the service of others were reinforced during every minute of the day. Learning how to never lose your keys came from my observations of the students' daily behaviors and practices.

Organization for my students was a crucial part of their day, not only because of the challenges they faced with their sight and autism, but also because they, like everyone I've ever met, wish to avoid being late, getting frustrated, or having their day derailed because of a misplaced key or other necessity.

Here are a few of the lessons I learned that helped me to always find my keys and other items of importance:

- Become a minimalist. My students identified what was essential and got rid of what wasn't. This reduced the clutter and rewarded them with time, less frustration, and a greater appreciation of what they had. Each of us can take some step today on mini-mizing our homes and work areas.

- Things of importance need a place of importance. My students put their keys in the exact same spot every day, immediately upon entering their room. Now I do the same. One hundred out of a hundred times my keys go into the exact same spot in my desk drawer. The exact same spot in my bag, same pocket in my jacket, and then back in the desk. Repeat after me, "Every thing has its place, every place has its thing."

- Two is one, and one is none. My students had a backup copy of their key stashed away in case of an emergency. They never needed it, but just in case they dropped one on a trip and couldn't find it, they had a built-in solution. Nice.

- Take responsibility. If something came up missing my students knew it was their responsibility. They never wasted time blaming someone else. Find it or move forward.

- Practice. The only way you will master organization is through practice. So, find out what is essential, assign it a place, make a copy if you can, take responsibility for what is yours, and practice until perfect.

I'm not going to pretend I never misplace an item, but on that extreme-ly rare occasion that I might, I will remember the tips I learned from my friends from Perkins.

Minimizing can arrive in many forms. I have friends who have lots of scraps of paper and sticky-notes with important numbers and infor-mation. They always seem to be searching for what they wrote down. I have simply my journal. Everything of importance goes in there. If it is important enough to be written down, it is important enough for my journal. (I do use some online storage areas like Evernote, DropBox and others, but nearly everything goes in the journal first.)

Kelly Croy

One more aspect to minimizing that has been incredibly helpful to me is understanding the following statement: **I have everything I need.** You really do. You really do have everything you need. Just as a little hickory nut shell has everything packed inside it to grow an enormous tree, so do you have everything you need to lead, write that novel, run that race, become your best. You don't really need that new software or computer. You really don't need a new suit or car. Sure, they would be nice. Keep things simple. Keep things minimal. You have all you need.

Wisdom is asking.

If you want something, start by asking. Assume the best first.

Many people claim they would give anything for a genuine opportunity to advance in life. I hear it all the time, "What I wouldn't do to have what she has!" or "Why does she have all the luck?" and even "I'm waiting for my ship to come in."

When an opportunity does present itself, however, it would seem only very few actually step forward. Why is that?

I believe it is because most people don't really want an opportunity, they want a reward. They want the pot of gold at the end of the rainbow, without participating in the adventure to locate it. They want the winning lottery ticket, the instant fix, or a wonder cure. They'd rather connect on a Hail Mary pass then drive the ball down the field, play by bone-smashing play. They would rather *wish* than work.

Opportunities and rewards are not the same.

An opportunity never arrives alone. It is always accompanied by work, sacrifice, and change.

Work deters a few from seizing an opportunity, but most people understand the basic idea that they have to put forth some effort to get something back. They just want to make certain the reward outweighs the effort. If it does they stay with it. If the reward isn't big enough, or if it arrives too late or too infrequently, they're gone. Sadly, most don't stick with an opportunity long enough to reap the benefits. Most often the reward is so close and is just around the next corner.

Sacrifice deters even more people from an opportunity than work. People are willing to put some time in for the reward, but they aren't always willing to give something up. Opportunity is always accompanied by sacrifice whether it be an investment of time, finances, or energy. The more comfortable we become in our lives the harder it is to make sacrifices for opportunities. Sacrifices can and should be made in balance with our values, and consideration for our family, but to be brutally honest, if you want something big, you must sacrifice something else.

Change is the biggest road block to opportunities because the thought of becoming something or someone new just out-right frightens people. People like who they are, and once they reach a certain age, they find an identity of comfort. (Tip: Don't ever get too comfortable.) They don't realize that change is actually growth, and growth is what life is all about. Once you stop growing, improving, and changing, the quest ends, the journey is over, and life loses its purpose. The conquering of every challenge creates a change. Opportunities change us for the better.

In your life you have been given many opportunities. You chased after some with full vigor. Some you sort of jogged after until they left your range of vision. Others zipped by without you even flinching. You have had opportunities, and you will have more.

The best advice I can offer is this: don't wait for opportunities to come to you. Figure out what you want, go after it, and make opportunities happen. Share your dreams. Ask for help. One of the greatest secrets of true wisdom is *asking*; so few actually do.

I have found that one of the wisest decisions I can make is to *simply ask*. Ask people to help. Ask people to take a look at something. Ask someone to consider giving you an opportunity. Ask for someone to consider giving you a discount. Whatever it is, whatever you need, ask. You will be surprised how often it is granted.

All of us should have dreams and all of us should be pursuing them. Sadly many people do not.

Now give. That's right. Think of ways *you* can offer genuine opportunities to others for no other reason than that you want someone to become all that they are capable of becoming. Do this and you will find opportunities at every turn in life. People love, respect, and reward those that help them.

There's something wrong with your dream.

There's something wrong with your television if you've spent more time in front of it than you have working at your dream. There's something wrong with your dream if you've spent more time with it than you have spent with your family.

Actually I'm wrong on both, and you know it. There is nothing wrong with your television nor your dream. You just need to prioritize and focus.

Prioritizing and focusing are two great disciplines. There are many books and blogs that can offer you advice on how to make some progress, but the truth is no one can do it for you.

You will not find time. You cannot make time. You can and should schedule time each day for your family and your dream.

Identify the bandits that steal your time from your family and your dream and launch a counter-attack. No dream needs to lie dormant until your children are raised. No family needs to be neglected while chasing a dream. You can and should work at both. Your life will be filled with purpose and fulfillment. Completion of your dream will benefit your family, in many ways, and your family can certainly help you in completing a dream, if nothing more than providing the much-needed drive.

Turn the television off, set the smart phone down, let your status update read: Please Stand By: Family Time or Please Stand By: Chasing a Dream, and then, and most importantly, actually do it.

Gain wisdom from mentoring.

We all need a Yoda. We can all be a Yoda.

Everytime I finish a mentoring session, I feel as if I learned more than I advised. The old adage holds true, "To teach is to learn twice." Mentoring is an ancient practice, and one I hope to encourage.

Some businesses and schools offer mentoring programs that pair newcomers or those who are struggling, with a more experienced individual. The programs certainly have their success, but there is something less than inspiring when the relationship is compulsory, or highly recommended. An ideal mentoring relationship occurs when one who truly aspires for advancement is matched with one who is willing and able to provide instruction and direction.

You may think you don't need a mentor, after all, you made it this far through hard work and discipline. Look how far you've come on your own! Who needs a mentor?

In this age of super-easy access to information, I fear we devalue experience, style, hindsight, and 'exceptions to the rule' that only a mentor can provide. A good mentor can provide you with feedback, instruction, and secrets, if you will, that would normally take you years to learn on your own, and forfeit your suffering through quite a few failures too. Don't worry. You'll still have your share of both, but the mentor will allow you to take the art to a new level. Sure, I can purchase books and DVDs on Wing Chun and learn a few moves that seemingly mirror those of Robert Downey Jr.'s fight scenes, but the real art of this ancient martial art cannot be summoned from independent learning. The same is true of all arts. Enter the mentor.

Mentoring in this age of social networking may occur to a degree through blog posts, articles, wikis, tweets, status updates, Skype video calls, websites, online videos, and emails, and that is a great start, but I am encouraging something more; a common time where a master unveils his secrets to a student privately. Two people agreeing to set aside an hour each week or so, to the advancement of the craft and the individual.

There is an unspoken covenant between the mentor and the student. *I am going to share with you all that I know. You will apply it, add to it, and pass it on to someone else.* The mentor doesn't hold back. The student doesn't shirk.

Two common problems occur today with mentoring. The first is that the student is embarrassed to admit what he does not know, and the second is that the mentor is embarrassed to admit what he does not know. (It seems everyone knows everything these days.) This must be overcome. Again: An ideal mentoring relationship occurs when one who truly aspires for advancement is matched with one who is willing and able to provide instruction and direction.

I am where I am today due to many mentors in my life. As a teacher, a coach, a father, a friend, an artist, a speaker, and a businessman, I now have opportunities to mentor others. I do not take them lightly. I do not think of myself a master of anything, and quite frankly the term mentor makes me feel old, but there is so much to be gained through mentoring. For me, I still have my mentors who I consult with, and I have my students that I meet with too. Successful mentoring is to not only be one, but to have one as well.

- How do you get a mentor? You find someone's work you admire, and you ask. Sound easy? Well, most people never ask.
- How do you become a mentor? Do great work. Wait for someone to ask. When they do… say, "yes."

Strengths and Weaknesses: Know Your Kryptonite

A wise man knows both his strengths and his weaknesses.

Our culture and history have provided us with some amazing heroes whose lessons serve to entertain, inspire, teach, and empower. Greek Mythology, the Bible, and even modern comics tell similar tales of heroes whose fate is determined by a single weakness.

The Greek hero Achilles was dipped into the fiery waters of the River Styx to make his skin impervious to any weapon in preparation for the Trojan War. His mother, a goddess, held onto his ankles while immersing him, and as a result his skin was untouched and unprotected where he was held. His enemies learned of his single weakness and volleys of arrows were launched at his ankles. Achilles was killed. Today we call a single point of vulnerability our Achilles Heel.

The Biblical story of Samson's strength is chronicled in the Book of Judges. Samson was able to wrestle a lion, destroy an entire army with the jawbone of an ass, and he even destroyed a temple of colossal size and structure. Samson too had but one weakness, the loss of his hair. Samson's girlfriend, Delilah, was bribed to uncover this weakness. After learning of it, she cut off his hair. He was weakened, blinded, and imprisoned.

Superman, arguably one of the best known heroes in modern culture, could fly, possessed enormous strength, had x-ray vision, shot heat-beams from his eyes, and bullets literally bounced off his skin. Superman, however, also had one weakness, kryptonite, a chunk of his home planet. When Superman came near the substance he would drop to his knees and become helpless.

Perhaps you are like me and your weakness is more likely procrastination than a meteorite from an alien world, a third piece of apple pie than an enemy's arrow, or an over-reaction than a monumental loss of strength from a bad haircut. Still, it is to our advantage and surely our responsibility to know what our weaknesses are and to guard against them.

We simply must take inventory of our weaknesses if we are to improve ourselves. Sadly, there are many that find little or no fault with their lives, and are one day suddenly blindsided. They are content by comparing themselves with only those who have worse faults. You can exercise for hours each day, but you won't see results until you overcome your desire to eat an entire chocolate cake for breakfast every morning. With self improvement comes self discipline, and another great benefit is, as we focus on improvement in one area, we gradually improve in several.

So, do you know your weaknesses? If not, how can you and your loved ones protect you from them? Each year I undergo a complete physical to help protect myself from illness. I do it as much for my family as I do for myself. Shouldn't we do the same for all of the important areas in our lives? Stand guard to attacks on your physical self, emotional self, financial self, spiritual self, and any area of your life that is important to you by simply identifying a danger.

We have seen so many fall from grace in Hollywood and in politics. We wonder how people can make such blunders, but realize they are caught up in their own self worth and success. They think they are unstoppable. They become arrogant. They become careless. The Greeks gave this extreme arrogance and over confidence its own word, Hubris. Hubris has plagued mankind for thousands of years. Guard yourself from Hubris.

We may not be heroes of paramount proportion, but we do have people counting on us and responsibilities to maintain. We must know our faults and weaknesses and work at improving upon them. We must hold ourselves accountable, share with a trusted accountability partner, and keep ourselves from those very temptations.

A steel worker knows his greatest vulnerability is a fall from a great height. He protects himself with a cable and harness, and works closely with coworkers to keep safety a top priority. During my years as a football coach we watched countless hours of film to not only learn of our opponents' weaknesses, but our own. It is time for you to take similar actions and reflections.

Let's take a quick inventory of some possible dangers that might be affecting key areas of your life just to get you started in the process: Are there actions you take at work that could endanger your job? Are there activities in your life keeping you away from loved ones? Do you indulge in certain foods or drinks that are hurting you physically? Is there an attack on your emotions that you need to confront? Are there people you need to avoid? Substances that bring out the worst in you? Are there places you visit that make you a less than ideal individual? Do you have an accountability partner that you can trust and bounce ideas off to help you improve? You get the idea. Maybe these could be added to your journal or discussed in private. Regardless, they make a great starting point.

Once you discover your vulnerabilities you will immediately start developing a plan of protection and escape. It is human nature. Having identified your weaknesses will take you further on the path to wisdom.

Fear not! Your friends and family are the ones who bring out the best in you, and they'll be there when you falter, as you will for them. The greater the problem, the greater the hero, so if your weakness is great, then great you will be, by overcoming it.

Make Your Day Great, Find your Kryptonite! You don't have to be the wisest to be the leader. Most leaders realize they are not the wisest even in their circle, but they know they are willing to be decisive and have the courage to take an idea, infuse it with wisdom, and work to make it a reality.

Wisdom will guide your ability to stay on course to fulfilling your organization's vision or your personal goals. I have dedicated an entire chapter to the leadership essential of vision. Wisdom is the guidance system that keeps you and your organization on course to your vision. Every decision you make as a leader brings you closer to your vision or further from your vision. Wisdom keeps you on track. Seek wisdom continuously.

Commitment 2

The Second Leadership Commitment
I will seek wisdom.

From this point forward, I will seek wisdom to become a better leader. I will read great books, surround myself with individuals who help me become a better leader, and I will reflect before I respond. I know wisdom is a continuing journey, and I will passionately pursue adding more wisdom to my leadership roles through a variety of sources.

CHAPTER 6

Tenacity

Be a contender. Enjoy the thrill of a challenge and competition.

Leaders finish what they start. They finish it even when doing so is no longer convenient and requires incredible effort.

It may require time, but a leader stays on course and sees projects and visions fulfilled. That is what separates a true leader from a boss or a manager. One of the most overlooked ingredients in leadership, and one of the most crucial measures of strong leaders is tenacity. Tenacity is a combination of perseverance, determination, grit, and stick-to-itiveness that makes leaders legendary for not having backed away from problems and challenges and always seeing the mission through no matter what!

Tenacity isn't a gift you are born with; it's a quality you develop over time. How do you acquire tenacity? Completing smaller tasks, and then completing larger tasks, and doing both with regularity. If you want to become good at quitting, practice quitting often with consistency. If you want to acquire tenacity practice sticking with tasks and goals through adversity and seeing them finished. Each time you complete a small task, the ability to complete larger tasks becomes easier. Each time you quit, quitting becomes easier too. We become what we consistently do.

Tenacity is the ingredient to becoming great. Tenacity is a mixture of desire and determination. You have to want something and then you have to want it badly enough to take action, and the final ingredient is repetition.

Tenacity = desire + action + repetition

Many people want something, but few ever take action to achieve it. They figure they either don't know enough or that it will take too long. They will make up one hundred excuses not to start. Others will start but get frustrated at some point and then quit. Very few will follow a dream all the way to completion. Those that do, build this crucial leadership trait of tenacity and become successful many times over. One success empowers the possibilities of future successes. One accomplishment actually makes it easier to complete future goals.

Leaders will face hard times. That's why we need leaders. They rise when others flee. They speak when others remain silent. Leaders need to possess the ability to keep going despite the odds. All of the other leadership traits are important, but if a leader hasn't been tested and shown tenacity there can be some doubt. I will take a leader who has persevered through a hardship over a leader that has never known adversity any day of the week. I admire tenacity.

Tenacity is all about taking action. You have to start somewhere. Just start!

> *"Heck, by the time a man scratches his behind, clears his throat, and tells me how smart he is, we've already wasted fifteen minutes."*
> **~ Lyndon Johnson**

You build tenacity like you do muscles. It takes time. It takes repetition. You must start somewhere.

No one becomes muscle-bound from going to the gym *once in awhile*. Consistency is the key. No one becomes 600 pounds overweight by eating a single box of doughnuts once in their life. Again, consistency is the key.

Everyone has a first time to the gym. It's awkward. You feel out of place. Keep going and pretty soon you build some clout. People start knowing your name. Continue your workouts with regularity and the other regulars start noticing you if you miss. Keep going and soon they notice your results. Enough trips over time and there is a change. The change isn't just physical. *You've* changed. The discipline of working out, getting out of bed, regularly scheduling time, permeates into other areas of your life. You begin to understand that commitment isn't just a word, it is the summation of your whole being.

Make commitments. Become committed.

Failure: I found out long ago that I simply cannot always be right. (You'd be surprised how many never make this important personal discovery.) I will make mistakes. I have decided, however, that the mistakes I do make will always be made in attempt to make a positive difference in the world. I also decided that I will never make the mistake of inaction. The worst mistake you can make in life is that of not acting.

There is no such thing as failure. There is only *eventually succeeding* after a series of failed attempts. You either eventually succeed or you quit. Success is that simple. Sure you must make changes, tweaks, and adjust your strategies. You can't expect to keep bulldozing the same ideas repeatedly. But do know, however, tenacity will eventually prevail. You cannot be denied as long as you keep trying. The only failure we can make is to make no attempt, or to quit trying. It's something we have heard many times, sure, but we need to keep reminding ourselves of this truth.

Becoming a successful leader is to enjoy the thrill of a challenge. That's what makes tenacity really work; you must enjoy tackling a challenge. There is a competitive nature inherent in building tenacity. Commitments matter to you. Finishing matters. Over time, even the struggle of battling procrastination and the temptation becomes appealing. That's tenacity at its best.

Building your tenacity ends procrastination. You make a decision and move forward with passion. This passion and tenacity go hand in hand. Your tenacity is fueled by the passion you have for what you are doing. A leader must have passion. A leader must genuinely care about the job he is doing, the organization he is serving, and the people he is leading and working alongside each day.

Abraham Lincoln A Role Model in Tenacity: Unquestionably, Abraham Lincoln is known throughout the world as one of the greatest leaders of all time. His list of accomplishments would be an impressive chore for several presidents let alone one. He is remembered for his accomplishments, not his failures, but without the latter, the former would have never happened. We must fail before we can succeed. Abraham Lincoln faced setbacks and defeat throughout his life. It is his perseverance that made him a great leader. He would not surrender to defeat. Lincoln understood one of the most important elements of leadership, the thrill of a challenge and the importance of tenacity.

When we think of Abraham Lincoln we think of his presidency, his memorial, his presence on our currency. But did you know Abraham Lincoln…

Was born into poverty.

Homeless at age seven.

Started working at the age of eight to support his family.

At nine, his mother died.

Failed in business more than once.

In his thirties, Lincoln borrowed money from a friend for a business venture, but within less than a year he was bankrupt. (It took him over sixteen years to pay back the debt.)

He decided to go to law school but was rejected.

Lincoln repeatedly ran for public office and lost. (He lost over eight elections.)

Eventually he met the love of his life and was engaged to be married, however his fiance' died. Lincoln suffered from a broken heart and then a nervous breakdown. He was even confined to a bed for six months.

Wow! I'd hate to face even one of those hardships!

At the age of 61 he ran for president. He won and became one of the greatest presidents in history. His presidency was plagued with challenges and temptations to quit, but he exhibited remarkable tenacity and refused to give in. The secret to his success? Tenacity.

Keep trying. Seek the thrill of a challenge.

Tenacity is needed in tough times and good times.

Tenacity. Know the word. Use it sparingly. Honor its meaning. Don't give up easily. Be persistent in your quest. You will encounter failures but you must be able to bounce back. A failure is simply a reminder to you that you are taking action and moving toward your goal. Tenacity takes confidence. Don't allow a failure to halt your momentum.

> *"Energy and persistence conquer all things."*
> **—Benjamin Franklin**

Here are eight actions to take when you are faced with a challenge:

1. **Remain confident**. Your confidence will serve you well and get you through hard times. You can't panic or worry. That's not what leaders do. If you are starting to feel that way, it's time for you to review your assets and visualize a successful outcome. If

at all possible find something good about what happened and make solving it admirable and if at all possible, fun. Remind yourself you are doing something and that something is better than nothing.

2. **Don't worry about embarrassment nor take it personally**. Time will wear those concerns away, and success will do the same even more quickly. Your energy should be spent on solutions. Worry robs us of our creativity and vitality. Change your thoughts from embarrassment to immediately visualizing the outcome you wanted. Recommit yourself to leading yourself and others to the solution. Review the failures of leadership mentors from history, books, and real life and know that you too will persevere in time.

3. **Focus and accept the problem.** Don't look for someone to pin this on nor pretend it's not actually happening. Leaders aren't looking for problems, but when one pops up they should be the first to identify and address them. Remember, you're not really a leader unless you are facing a problem. The rest of the time you are just a person with a title. Greek and Roman myths teach us much and one point is clear: the bigger the problem the greater the hero. No one became a legend for swatting a fly or crossing the street.

4. **Rally the team.** Yes, you are the leader, but you don't face challenges alone. (Would you accept all of the credit of a success?) Now is the time for you to call your advisors forward and get help from your team and network. You are surrounded by people that *can* help and *want* to help. You need to delegate responsibilities and keep everyone focused. You don't have to be a complete original. Review the vision. Get your team figuring out who has successfully dealt with this problem and see if it

will work for you. Pick up the phone. Bring them on board as a consultant. Leaders maximize the utilization of all of the resources they have in confronting a challenge.

5. **Formulate and communicate the plan.** In times of crisis it is best to figure out who needs to know what is going on and inform them. That list must include those that will be impacted negatively despite how uncomfortable it may feel. Be flexible. In times of challenges and crisis you must keep the lines of communication open and be willing to try multiple tactics or new approaches. Remind everyone of their role and check in with them often. Keep everyone focused on the plan not the dire consequences. Communicate how awesome it will be once we have weathered this storm and how it will prepare all for future battles. This is what leadership is all about.

6. **Take action!** Hoping the problem goes away is meaningless. Get involved and get after it. Make certain that you, the leader, are involved in the work, especially some of the unpopular jobs. Doing so will invigorate your team. This is where you set the example for everyone to follow. How you deal with the crisis verbally, physically, emotionally, and professionally sets the tone and example for others to follow. Choose wisely.

7. **Evaluate your outcomes.** What is working? Should you try something else? Are your resources and team being utilized effectively? What do we need to start doing, keep doing, and stop doing? You need feedback. Get some new perspectives and generate authentic statistics.

8. **Repeat steps 1-7.** Tenacity is all about the repetition of what works and the avoidance of what doesn't work. You have to repeat the actions that provide success and discipline yourself to stay away from actions that are ineffective or wasteful.

How to build tenacity.

Tenacity isn't something we are born with as a baby. Some children might be a little more stubborn than others, but the ability to apply it to situations and persevere is developed over time through repeatedly choosing to do the hard work.

The question you ask then is, "How do I develop my tenacity? Stick-to-it-tiveness? Perseverence?"

The answer lies in how you react to every challenge brought before you no matter how big or small. You don't need to conquer every single challenge immediately, and make each a tremendous success, but, by making *some* progress, taking *some* action, making *some* advancement, sticking with something a *little longer than it is comfortable* truly builds tenacity.

Take dieting for example. Most people throw in the towel when they momentarily step outside their limits and engage in a brief moment of a sumo-wrestler-free-for-all buffet. Whoops! A one-time breach of discipline and they quit. Tenacity in action would allow them to admit the mistake and see the diet through with its mistakes and setbacks. Tenacity would keep them from throwing in the towel and get them to realign, refocus, and continue onward to their goal. Leadership is about understanding that there will always be mistakes. Leadership is knowing that mistakes remind you that you are on the right path to success. Leadership is knowing how to respond to these very necessary mistakes as we follow the vision. Mistakes are road signs that should be read as, *Rough Road Ahead! Keep Going! You're on the Right Path!*

A leader responds by celebrating the mistake with the team and adding it as one of the variables to the overall plan. "Sure, we didn't see this one originally, but look what we have learned! Imagine how much stronger we are going to be knowing this! Let's all make sure we know what to do in case we encounter this problem again, and see if we can improve upon our end result." Leaders respond to problems, they don't react.

Strengthening your tenacity.

I am an advocate of journaling. You will see many, many references to it in this book. By journaling your decision making process and responses to challenges, you will see how you are building your tenacity and where you need to improve. To me, a former coach, reviewing journal entries is the equivalent of watching film. Coaches watch lots of film. It tells them what they did well, and where they are vulnerable. It is the first step in creating the plan.

The old-fashioned to-do list is a great way to build tenacity too. You know the drill. Write down the things you need to do and start crossing them off. Hold yourself accountable to the tasks and goals you set. From there you can graduate to monthly and yearly resolutions. It really works.

Personal accomplishments and physical achievements also build tenacity. There is a correlation between the discipline of working out and following through on professional and personal goals. That discipline of following a physical regimen translates over to other areas in your life. You reap the benefits in other areas when you build tenacity in one. So, set goals in many different areas, especially the ones you enjoy, and see the benefits accumulate where you least expected. Choose some big goals. Sign up to run a race. Get up early to workout or write. This is leadership cross training!

Keeping your word and being genuinely authentic is a great way to build tenacity. When you promise someone you will help them and you follow through, you build character and trust, and it transfers over to other areas of your life. It helps you become a better leader in many ways. Doing what we promise, especially when we'd rather be doing something easier and more fun, really builds that one-of a-kind level of tenacity that everyone admires.

Discipline is the primary element of tenacity. Outlined in the examples above you now understand that tenacity is all about taking action and becoming disciplined. Find areas in your life that need a little more discipline and this will build your overall tenacity and help you become a great leader.

Being goal-oriented is an important part of building tenacity. Truly, without goals it will be difficult to measure and know what you are working toward. I am firmly convinced that even the goal setting I did as a boy in the Scouts has helped me to build the character and follow-through that I have today. Every action we commit ourselves to and follow-through to accomplishing matters.

Ways to Build Your Tenacity

1. Create to-do lists.
2. Set New Year's Resolutions.
3. Meet with an accountability partner.
4. Journal.
5. Schedule monthly meetings with your goals.
6. Follow-through on your promises.

The Easiest Way to Build Tenacity: We write down the groceries we need, gifts to buy at the mall, doctors' appointments, to-do lists, recipes, directions, car maintenance appointments, and other things we deem important. We compose emails, texts, Twitter posts, blogs, and we update our Facebook status with regularity. Yet, most people choose not to write down their goals, their resolutions, or what they want to accomplish for the year, yet alone their life. They fail to design a plan, or even make a list of where they'd like to go, what they'd they like to have, who they'd like to help, or the person they'd like to become, and then they're frequently disappointed when life doesn't deliver their dreams and wishes.

Writing down our goals and resolutions matters. Follow the recipe to create the dish, arrive at the location, assemble the product, complete the course. It really is that simple.

My goals, resolutions, and plans are always updated in a small portable journal. I take it nearly everywhere I go. There are no scrap pieces of paper in my life, no post-it notes, no napkin designs; I write everything in my journal. If I want to change direction, need a little motivation, or can't remember where I was on a project, I know where to find it.

Writing down the actions I need to take and have accomplished helps me stay focused and motivated to complete more. I have found few other actions as important to building my personal leadership abilities as writing everything down in a journal.

I also begin each day with an index card that serves as my to-do list. It works in conjunction with my journal. Neither are difficult, nor take up much time. They work well for me, but perhaps not you, and that's fine. All I wish to accomplish is to emphasize the importance of writing down your goals and resolutions. That's it.

Just jot some ideas down after some thought and review them periodically as the very minimum to make some awesome accomplishments. Or, start a journal, and design the life you want to live.

Of course for further proof there is the most cited study of all time about writing down your goals. The Harvard Study on writing down goals is powerful. It states that 3% of the graduates who took the time to write down what they wanted, accomplished more than the other 97% combined. Wow!

My personal testimony: Writing down my goals and resolutions has created incredible results in my life. Without question, journaling is the single most important tool in my arsenal. Before you dismiss it as something you just aren't interested in I urge you to try it. You'd be surprised by those of whom you admire who keep a journal. If you already keep a journal consider taking it up a notch and find new ways it can add value to your life.

For those that don't know where to begin, I encourage you to begin simply. There is no right or wrong method for journaling. If you workout every day your body is going to change, regardless if you know what you're doing or not. The better the plan, the better the results. The same is true for writing down and maintaining your goals in life. *Some* is better than *none*.

I often record what exercise I did or what I have recently written or read. If I see an inspiring quote I record it. Special moments with my family, personal achievements, and setbacks all make it in the journal. There is no wrong way to begin, and you will quickly see its value as you review your comments from time to time. You will build a passion to complete and achieve as you set tasks, goals, and resolutions. You will develop the habits of leadership.

Is There Really Time for That?

For those that say they don't have time to write down their goals, please know that our time here is short and we need to spend it on what matters most. Take a few minutes to design the life you want and aim yourself in that direction.

Q: **How do I build tenacity *each day*?**

A: **Do *Some*!**

Each and every day I take out a small index card and make my to-do list. The result is simple; I get things done.

Each year I set goals for myself and monitor them regularly in my journal. The result is always positive; I accomplish some great goals each year.

Still, there are some tasks that either evade me, or I am avoiding, and some BIG life goals that I cannot even seem to get started. With these, I seem to be in a rut. I continually write them down as 'to-do' but barely make any progress. Unfortunately, the reality is that these are the goals and accomplishments that would mean the most to me if completed. They would make the biggest impact in my life.

I have always read and heard that you need to write goals down and that they need to be specific. Most of the time that works well for me, but recently I have uncovered a secret that has allowed me to make progress in those really tough areas that I have been stagnant for so long.

The solution is: *some*. That's right, just do *some*.

A novel can be 60,000 words. You can't write one of those in a day.

Ten pounds is 35,000 calories. You won't be losing that in a day.

Too often the knowledge of 'the amount' it takes to finish prevents us from starting or staying on track.

We surrender out of fear of failure and convince ourselves with the improbability of success or imagine the exhaustive state we will be at, even with a fraction of the progress.

That is why most people don't write novels or ever lose that ten pounds.

I recently discovered this amazing adjective called *some*. It's not scary, and it's barely even measurable, yet with it you can get anywhere and accomplish anything.

Can't run a marathon? Great, run *some*.

Can't reduce your diet down to 1800 calories a day? Super! Just reduce it by *some*.

Some allows us to reach our goals. *Some* allows us to make progress.

The only thing that must accompany *some* to make it happen is the noun **consistency**.

Kelly Croy

Do *some* **every** day.

Motivation and Tenacity Go Hand in Hand! One day I picked up my daughter's basketball near where she practices at home. It was as smooth as an apple. Useless. All the bounce was gone, and it was becoming threadbare in some areas. I was about to toss it in the trashcan and get her a new one when my daughter stopped me. She told me she was taking it to practice with her that day and that her coach would give her a new basketball. In fact, she elaborated, her coach would give her a new basketball for every one she wore out. Wow! What a fabulous idea!

My daughter's coach did in fact give her a basketball for every one she wore out, but more amazing than that is that her coach instilled in her a desire to practice, gave her a visual goal, and reinforced the successful habits of a committed athlete. Well done.

I incorporated that idea into my own life. I have been wanting a new laptop for some time. Not just any laptop, but the new MacBook Air from Apple. I have saved my money and all I need to do is place the order, but I made a commitment to myself to wait until I have finished the book I have been working on for the past two years. My current laptop used for writing will be replaced with the new one when the book is finished and query letters mailed.

It's easy to become distracted, but there are techniques we can employ to counter them and become more productive, and I believe creating your own buy-back program is an excellent idea to meet your goals. Tenacity has its enemies like distraction and procrastination that we must conquer.

Discipline, focus, commitment, and training are the keys to success in any area in life, whether it be writing, sports, or art. The distractions become less influential when we have a clear measurable goal in front of us.

I hope you can find an area in your life that you can set-up a similar buy-back reward program. Perhaps you can use it with a friend or family member, or perhaps even with yourself to build this ever-important leadership trait of tenacity.

Rudy Ruettiger and Kelly Croy

Rudy Ruettiger is one of the most tenacious leaders I have ever met. His real life, never-give-up mantra was made into one of my favorite movies, *Rudy*. His story of tenacity has inspired generations of leaders.

•••

I decided early in this life that I cannot possibly be right 100% of the time, and probably won't even be right half of the time. I cannot control what other people think about me. I will make mistakes, but I will not allow that to deter me from taking action.

The contents of this book may very well be a turning point for those who apply what they read, but unless you do something with it and take action you will never be a true leader. Sure, you will have learned a lot about leadership. You will have the knowledge, you will know the steps, you will be prepared, but actually making the decisions and taking the necessary steps is the hallmark of a leader. Once you start, however, each action builds onto the next, building momentum and with that momentum future actions and decisions become easier and easier.

Don't be the 'Monday Morning Quarterback' that always voices their opinion on what *should have happened*. Anybody can look back and tell you what the proper course *should* have been. It's the forward thinking leader, that must take the action that will impact not only the lives of those in the present, but also, and maybe even more importantly, of those yet to arrive. That's leadership. Foresight!

Your life will not be defined by chance; it will be defined by choice. Choose wisely. Do BIG things. Strive to make a difference in the lives of others. Above all, take action. Don't aim for perfection. Aim for progress. If the number one is greater than zero, then doing something, regardless of how small, is greater than doing nothing. Start.

> *"The most difficult thing is the decision to act, the rest is merely tenacity."*
> **~Ameilia Earhart**

Don't confuse leading with managing. Don't confuse leading with holding an office or position. Leaders don't entertain, "What's the least I can do?" What's in it for me?" They focus on, "How can I make this happen? Who can I help? What difference can I make?" Managers, good managers, keep operations going, perhaps win some games, or make a profit. Leaders in contrast create what has never been before. Leaders create a new experience. Leaders take us where we have not been.

Leaders inspire and help others become self-motivating. The un-inspired seldom do extraordinary things in extraordinary ways. Get people to do ordinary things in extraordinary ways. Get people to attempt the extraordinary. Leaders keep everyone invigorated, excited, and focused.

Leaders don't wait until they are elected or appointed. They aren't waiting for someone to say, "Go!"

A leader must know what needs to be done next. A leader needs to know how to launch a project, how to regroup from a setback or failure, how to celebrate a victory. There is much a leader must know, but that knowledge takes the back seat to what a leader must do!

Yes, you actually have to accomplish something.

"Innovation distinguishes between a leader and a follower."
-Steve Jobs

Leadership is about accomplishments. A leader will fail, fail, fail, and fail again, but eventually a success will come, and that success will be the measurement of her leadership. A leader should be remembered by their greatest success, not their failures, but in the modern age of hype and sensationalism this isn't always immediately true. Still, over time, I believe success always outshines failures. A person should always be measured on their best accomplishment, not their most glaring fault. I can think of but a few exceptions to this belief; a leader who intentionally misuses a position of leadership will and should be remembered for their selfish and damaging acts.

A leader must make a contribution. I call this contribution an achievement. It is as true now as it was 3000 years ago. To be a successful leader at some point you must achieve something.

A boss and a manager are not held to this same standard. A boss and a manager can be quite successful without ever achieving anything. They can maintain, organize, or just keep things afloat. But not a leader. Leadership is about progress. Leadership is about giving more than was expected.

Before focusing on obtaining achievements I really want to be clear that the path to excellence is filled with failures. You know how to achieve something don't you? It's simple; never give up. Fail. Fail. Fail. Fail. Fail. Fail. Fail. And fail again. Keep failing and eventually you will achieve something. You will have contributed. You will have led.

Perhaps you will be a great leader and only fail as half as much as the rest of the leaders, and that is fine, but know that you will fail. Know that you must fail. You don't have to like it nor make a habit of it, but the road to success is full of failures. Celebrate them. Learn from them. Reflect upon them, but move on.

You cannot be content with just reading books about leadership. You cannot call yourself a leader even when the title or position is bestowed upon you. Eventually you have to do something, and eventually the something you do must result in an achievement.

> *"Let me tell you the secret that has led me to my goal. My strength lies solely in my tenacity."*
> **~Louis Pasteur**

As Seth Godin says, "*You Must Ship.*"

The starting point of anything can be a little intimidating, especially if it's your first time.

If it's a race, you might compare yourself to other runners, question the course, or start predicting what could go wrong. If it's a financial goal, your initial deposit may look so minuscule in comparison to the total amount needed that you begin to second guess even starting.

Goals, resolutions, and habits are what transform us and bring out the best in us, but they really don't need to be complex and stressful.

They need to be fun and engaging.

Run your race, not the guy's next to you. Plan your financial portfolio, not your coworkers'. Create your plan and personalize your goals with your life.

A new year, a birthday, the start of the month, even the first day of the week can provide us with an opportunity to begin something new, begin something needed, and chart a new course. It's nice to have those clean-slate moments on the calendar. Embrace them. Use them to your advantage! It's also important to remember, *any time* is a good time to start something worthwhile.

Most people abandon a resolution because they mess up and ruin a 'perfect run' of the habit they wanted to create. Well, don't worry. You're going to mess up, miss a day, and make a mistake. That's part of the success formula.

> *"Patience and tenacity of purpose are worth more than twice their weight of cleverness."*
> **~Thomas Henry Huxley**

The secret to successful resolutions is what you do after you had a setback. You just start again. It really is that simple, but so many fail because they refuse to begin again.

Edison's 10,000 lightbulb filament failures, and Disney's 300 failed attempts to find a financial backer, combined with every person who's ever lost weight, quit an addiction, destroyed debt, or ran a race will remind us that setbacks will occur and we must persist. Failure is a key ingredient.

When you fail, give yourself an opportunity to adjust, make corrections, and set a new course. Perhaps you need to consult someone who has had some success in this area, but don't wait. Keep failing. Keep collecting data. Keep trying. Never wait until you have the equipment, money or time, because you never will. Just start.

I am firmly convinced that if you make 364 attempts at anything, by the 365th you're going to be pretty darn good at it and see some major accomplishments. Of course it doesn't have to be that many days. Work on building consistency. Work on building tenacity. Even after a few consistent attempts you will begin to see improvement.

Leaders Get Rid of 'The Crappy Stuff': When CEO Mark Parker of Nike called Apple CEO Steve Jobs for advice, Jobs told him to "get rid of the crappy stuff."

According to Forbes, When Parker asked for advice, Jobs said: "Well, just one thing. Nike makes some of the best products in the world. Products that you lust after. But you also make a lot of crap. Just get rid of the crappy stuff and focus on the good stuff." Leaders make a difference in the lives of others and the world. They do what has not been done before. They take people to new places. Leaders create meaningful experiences. To accomplish this, however, leaders can't be tenacious about everything; they must focus on what matters. Take Steve Jobs's advice to heart: identify the crappy stuff and let it go. Focus on what will produce results. Focus on what matters.

One of the most important things a leader must do is identify what they shouldn't do. Don't try to do everything. Learn to say, "No." Be proud of what you do, but be prouder of what you didn't do. There is much wisdom in these words.

"What lies behind us and what lies before us are tiny matters compared to what lies within us."
~Walt Emerson

How do Leaders Run a Meeting?

To keep things flowing and moving really consider if a meeting is necessary. If this is something that can be accomplished in an email or some other communication, do that first. Try to meet with people individually, but if you have to call everyone together for a formal meeting follow these rules:

1. **There's always a meeting before the meeting.** The leader should meet with key people and walk them through what outcomes are wanted at the meeting.

2. **Keep a firm outline**. Don't read a handout to those in a meeting. Everyone hates that.

3. **Stick to the Clock.** Meetings should begin on time. Be short. End on time.

4. **A meeting should have a beginning, a middle, and an end.** The beginning is a short recap of why we are here, and what we hope to accomplish. The middle is the meat of the problems and solutions that need to be addressed. That's why you are here. The closing is the challenge and goal setting to everyone in the room. Setting clear objectives, measurable progress, by certain dates. When we meet again, we want these numbers improved. Everyone should leave knowing what is expected of them individually and as a team as a whole. Everyone should have a homework assignment for the next meeting.

5. **How to handle questions.** Questions should be asked in private after the meeting if they are personal. Ask if anyone has an urgent question that must be answered now. If not, let's followup with an email or a personal conversation after the meeting.

6. **Truly respect everyone's time.** Keep the meeting as short as possible and don't let others drag it on. Post what was discussed and determined in some fashion and include what is expected and by when.

Why doesn't someone take action? I fear the number one reason people do not take action and accomplish more is that they fear what others think. A leader must overcome this! Be loyal to virtues and your vision. Your friends, and those that matter, will respect and love you for it. You will always have critics, especially as a leader. Welcome them. If your critics are virtuous and share a like-minded vision, then take their comments into consideration. If they lack character and integrity, or are following a different vision, take their comments in stride and shrug it off.

What do you allow to influence your decisions? What is your creed? When I was in college I took out a piece of paper and wrote Croy's Creed. On it, I listed what was important to me. I have been fine tuning it my entire life. Who matters? I love the creed of "God and Country". I have shared this with many students over the years, and we have had great discussions. Many have argued, unsuccessfully to me, that their family should be placed ahead of these. I have tried to explain that for me, the hierarchy of valuation is in the following order:

God matters.

Your country matters.

Your personal integrity matters.

Your family matters!

You health matters.

Then everything else.

The creed I follow is influenced by my faith, the leaders I admire and the books I read. My vision of my future also influenced my creed heavily. What are your priorities? You don't have to agree or adopt mine, but think about why I have may adopted this order of importance and how I live my life might change when the order changes. How we think about our values and priorities will impact our tenacity. If we are unclear then we certainly cannot adopt or apply tenacity. Clarity is power. I will be focusing an entire chapter of this book on vision. We will cover vision in great detail.

Inspire others with your tremendous activity and unwavering character and discipline. Too many don't decide. They live in that grey area of, "Should I? Or Shouldn't I?" Taking action is conquering fear. There are no right or wrong choices if you follow the six elements of leadership emphasized in this book. Your decisions should be executed with wisdom, the right attitude, with tenacity, with clear communication, with authenticity, and with a daring vision. How can you go wrong?! You will not fail.

"What's Next?" Is there a marathon in your future? Certification? A trip? A new house? A book?

Asking, "What's next?" can be an incredibly powerful, perhaps even a life-changing question. A question that can change the quality of your life. A question that can change your purpose, perhaps even create your legacy. Too often the question is either avoided completely or embraced too quickly.

Some people ask, "What's next?" with excitement and anticipation. Others avoid it outright.

Avoidance: Why are some people afraid to ask, "What's Next?" Perhaps they are comfortable and complacent where they are and they don't want to disrupt that false sense of security. They live in their past accomplishments, and talk about what they have achieved. Everyone should celebrate their victories in life, but everyone needs to move on to a new challenge sooner than later. Asking, "What's next?" creates progress and forward movement, and it's fun. Sitting down and planning your next big move, goal, event, project, race, or plan is excitement-building time. I love these creative periods of brainstorming and envisioning.

Contentment: A friend of mine tells me he is content. He believes 'what's next' will *find him* when the time is right. In the meantime he relishes in his stories of past accomplishments. I understand that, because he really has accomplished much, but for me I must ask what's next and seek it out. Life is short and I want to make the most of it.

When opportunity presents itself, I will pounce on it. In the meantime, I will be attempting to make my own luck in this world. I will show gratitude, I will be thankful, but I will not be content. There is too much in this world to do. I am thankful for the innovators before me who were not content. Mother Theresa could have stopped her life of service in her sixties but she didn't, and that made all the difference.

Are your greatest days in front of you or behind you? It doesn't matter how old you are or your physical status. You can accomplish great things and you should be asking what's next.

Premature: Some people ask "What's next?" prematurely. I suffer from this. I am always anxious to move on to the next BIG thing, sometimes my energy shifts before I have completed an important project. What's next is powerful and important, but it has its place and time. Make sure you finish up your project or dream before moving on too quickly. You can maintain those great ideas and finish what you've already started, and prepare to ask yourself, "What's next?"

Magic Hour: The best time to begin envisioning what you will do next is not after you accomplish your current goal or project, but as you enter the final finishing stages. Hemingway always abandoned his writing for the day mid-sentence to keep himself fresh and eager to dive back into his writing when he returned.

I know I must sign-up for another athletic event before I finish competing in my current race or I will get a touch of the blues and fall out of training. I know my wife always enjoys looking forward to a trip, so we plan ahead. Even Apple has a pipeline of "what's next" products they are preparing. You should have a list ready in your journal and actually begin working on it as you finish your latest and greatest life victory.

It's Not Time for That: A good friend of mine is a successful writer and speaker. His books quite simply change lives. An aspiration for any writer. An aspiration for any speaker. An aspiration for any person.

Every now and then I contact my friend with an idea that I truly believe he must act on immediately. He casually responds nearly every time with, "Great idea, but it's not time for that yet."

Brilliance.

I'm blessed with Attention Deficit Disorder, better known to all as ADD. Blessed? Yes, because it is one of the muses that feeds me such creative, out-of-this-world ideas. I love it. One of the drawbacks, however, is of course the fact that I get so many ideas that I want to jump from project to project and then I don't finish things. I never, ever, refer to my ADD as anything but a blessing. I mean that. It's as much a part of me as my blue eyes. In fact, I try not to refer to my ADD at all. (I love it so much I feel it's like bragging about how much you can bench press. After all, I consider ADD one of my super powers, but like all powers it needs to be controlled.)

When all of these creative ideas start flooding my brain and pushing out the project that I really need to buckle-down on and finish, I just need to remind myself that it's not time for that, yet. And I do. My brain starts screaming, "Let's do this!" I just say to myself, "It's not time for that brain." I take out my journal and I write down the amazing idea that just popped in there. I date it. Sometimes I even do a very quick sketch or two of what it's suppose to look like or do. I give the idea a bold heading so when I flip through my journal I see it. *Then I skip a line or two and write why I need to return to the project I interrupted and what it will mean to me and my family when I am finished.*

It's very important that you complete that last step. Once that new idea pops into your brain it steals some of the excitement and energy from the project you are working on. You have to invigorate that passion and energy back into your project again. You will need to recapture that purpose and energy. Then immediately jump back into that project and make some real progress. Remind yourself of why you want to finish, what it will mean, and the date you want it completed. *Being successful is not just knowing what to do, but knowing when to do it.*

Here are the steps to take when your project gets interrupted by a new, wonderful idea:

1. Remind yourself, "It's not time for that, yet."
2. Take out your journal and write down your new idea quickly with a big, bold heading, and a quick sketch if needed.
3. Reinvigorate your current project with a brief journal entry highlighting your passion, interest, and what it means to complete.
4. Dive right back into the project you were working on knowing the epiphany you just had is safely locked away and won't be lost.
5. Use visualization and self-talk to restart the project and regain your energy and commitment.

Finish that project. Everyone loves and respects those who do what they say, and follow-through on their dreams and ideas. Again, as Seth Godin and Steve Jobs love to remind us, "Real Artists Ship!" Walk your talk. Dream big, but finish!

"A river cuts through rock, not because of its power, but because of its persistence."
~Jim Watkins

Keep Yourself Accountable: My recent natural gas bill arrived. While bills are my least favorite piece of correspondence each month, I have to admit the helpfulness of the statement. It included a nice graph of my usage over the last year. It let me know how much I have paid and what I owe. Interestingly enough, it even predicted my usage for the following month. Each statement serves as a reminder and holds us to a certain level of accountability of what we owe. It lets us know where we are.

Wouldn't it be great if we received a similar billing statement each month for our goals?

Seriously! Most people never know where they are with the goals they wish to accomplish. It would be awesome to receive a statement each month telling us how much time we've put into our dream, what we owe, where we are at, and what we need to finally finish it.

Well, we can. My billing statement each month is in my journal. I choose the 28th of each month as the due date for my dream statements because I was born on the 28th of July and that's the easiest day for me to remember. It's like a private monthly celebration of my life and what I plan to do with it.

You can do the same.

You see, if we don't review our life goals regularly we get behind, just like we would with a real bill. Unlike the natural gas company, we won't receive any late notices, but what we owe starts piling up. Most of the time what we owe starts piling up to a level that makes it appear impossible to accomplish. That's why people quit. Can you imagine how hard it would be if you tried to pay two months at a time, or your entire yearly bill all at once? Ouch! The same is true of our goals and dreams.

Just like our billing statements from our utilities we need to make monthly contributions and track our progress. I started an online Spanish course with www.duolino.com and a course in computer programming at www.codeacademy.com. They award me badges for my progress and send me reminders via email to get back at it. We need these reminders of where we are at in life. If you can afford a personal life coach, trainer, or personal assistant, great, if not, build the tenacity and gumption to create your own billing statement.

So, bust out that journal daily or weekly if you can, but especially on the date of your birth each month. Create a reminder or alert on your phone or calendar if needed.

Keep Momentum by Celebrating Small Victories

It can be challenging to keep your momentum going. Chunk out smaller goals and celebrate each accomplishment. Then dive right in and finish! The longer something takes the more unlikely it is that you will finish.

Write down the big three questions that will drive you toward success:

1. What do I need to continue doing?
2. What do I need to start doing?
3. What do I need to stop doing?

Trying vs. Training: Or How to Win at Anything! I often don't know what to say when someone tells me they've quit. It's one of those rare moments when I'm speechless.

I grew up in a house where you either succeeded, or you weren't finished yet. There was no happy middle ground. Homework was either completed or I was working on it. The option of not completing it never entered my mind.

Sports further emphasized this point. I could not imagine going to my coach and telling him, "Well, I tried, but I just couldn't get the job done. I'm gonna stop now. No more for me, thank you. I've had my share. Sorry it didn't work out."

Nope. No way! I'd never say that! I'd rather walk into a bear's den beating a pot with a metal spoon with a raw piece of meat tied around my neck than do that. It's just not happening.

I apply the same tenacity to my life. I am either achieving what I set out to do, or I am not finished. It's that simple. I think it can be best summed up in the idea of trying vs. training.

Trying sounds okay when you first say it. "Sure, I'll give it a try." It's innocent. You'll do your best. The problem with trying though is that it leaves that other option out in the open. The other option being that you can walk away if it doesn't work out.

Training on the other hand takes that other option right off the table. Training is an entirely different matter. For starters, there is a plan. You know what you are going to do to make it happen. No wild swings. No shooting from the hip. When you train, you measure your progress, make sure you're on track, and you use every resource you can to achieve success. When you train, you discipline yourself and follow a set of rules or guidelines.

See the difference? Training and trying are not the same. Trying is a half-hearted effort. Training is focused on a result. Those who try sometimes get lucky and make it. Those who train make it every time. It might take awhile, but they *will* get there. Training lasts until there is eventual success. Trying allows the option to exit at anytime.

Imagine, if you will, that you are given the amazing opportunity to win a million dollars during an NBA halftime show by shooting three foul shots. Make three in a row and you win a million dollars. The contest will be televised live in three weeks. Would you try to make the shots or would you train to make the shots? I'd train! You'd find me out on the playground basketball court late at night, even if it was raining, practicing those shots. I'd read books about the psychology of performing under pressure. I'd watch videos. I'd consult coaches. And let me tell you this... I'd win. I'd win because I'd train!

Our journey in life is no different. Do you have a plan? An accountability partner? Are you focused? Do you miss practices? Are you disciplining yourself? Ultimately, the question for the leader is, do you have **tenacity**?

So, how do you win a million dollars shooting a basketball free throw? Simple. You train. Tenacity is built alongside everything you train for in life, and our lives are certainly worth more than a million dollars.

"We may encounter many defeats, but we must not be defeated."
~ **Maya Angelou**

Advertisers Use Tenacity and You Should Too! Each year I am amazed at the increased marketing for Christmas. Advertisements galore! I am delivered enough Christmas catalogs and advertisements in a year to litter-train all of the 101 Dalmatians. Some of the advertisements arrive in September! But it doesn't stop there. There has been an increase of Christmas marketing in my email, on my television, and everywhere I go. We laugh each year and note how early the marketing begins.

Marketing! Advertisements! Commercials! Sales! Fliers! Discounts! Specials! Deals!

So much marketing!

Why do they do it?

It's *simple*. Marketing works.

I could protest, shun it, and write countless pages about the absurdity of so much marketing. I could interview my poor mailman and retell his woes of the literal heaviness of delivering these must-have reminders for sales, gadgets, and discounts. But in the end, they will still arrive, because when it's all said and done, they are effective. Again, marketing works.

Surrender? No, never surrender. In fact, I recommend the opposite; join them. That's right. Become a relentless broadcaster of something timeless and meaningful. Market to yourself. Send meaningful messages to yourself about something that truly enhances and encourages self improvement and leadership. Create advertisements for yourself about accomplishing much!

It would be great if one phone call or note was enough, but it's not. We learn that from our advertisers. How many times do you receive the exact same advertisement? Me too. Crazy, isn't it?! (Remember though, it works.) No, we need you to say and do lots of encouraging things. Repeatedly.

Marketers have a mission behind their madness; they want to close a sale. You need a goal behind your marketing of leadership and personal development. I suggest starting small. Let's start with reminding yourself throughout the day of keeping the proper attitude of a leader, or the need to seek wisdom to become a great leader, or to continue your thirst for tenacity in becoming your best. Market the ideas in this book to yourself and others regularly.

I love little notes of encouragement. Positive quotes inspire me. A voicemail from a friend makes my day. Emails from a friend with encouragement are a treasure. In fact, anytime someone reaches out to me with the intention of goodwill, it makes my day. I'm sure the same holds true for you. I'm sure the same is true for those you love.

Be relentless. Find creative ways to remind yourself to stay on track. That is the key to tenacity; you must advertise the importance of staying the course.

Mentors Can Help You Stay on Track!

When I was little I had a goldfish. He didn't last long. I overfed him. He died getting too much of a good thing. The food poisoned his water.

I got a second goldfish. This time my sister was assigned the job of monitoring my care of the little guy; he lasted considerably longer.

Sometimes in life we need an accountability partner that keeps us on the right path. They help us stay true to our dream, our goal, our creed. An accountability partner by nature is a boost to our tenacity and productivity. Leaders need mentors and accountability partners.

Kelly Croy

Some call them their counsel or advisors. Regardless, having such partners in life are a boost to both your wisdom and tenacity.

An ideal accountability partner is someone that will be honest with you. They have the courage to correct you when you are out of line. They hold you to a high standard. They ask tough questions. They can humble themselves enough to compliment and encourage. They call you out when you need it, and they defend you when you're right. They check in on you, whether you like it or not. They will not let you walk down the wrong path. They will not let you quit. With them you become better.

This is a tall task to ask of anyone. So, don't ask.

I have numerous accountability partners. It seems I have one for nearly every interest. I have a buddy I workout with, and he encourages me to do better physically. I have other friends that help me along my spiritual journey. They send me words of wisdom and encouragement, especially when I am down or in a dark place. I have accountability partners that check on my writing progress, my art, and even my marketing and finances. They encourage me to do more, be more, become more. And, I asked none of them to do it.

The accountability partners you need in your life are already in position. They have been with you for years. You either are, or are not, listening to them. If you are sure you don't have any, stop, and listen harder. They're there. They're the ones telling you whether you are enjoying too much of a good thing or not doing enough. Listen to them.

Accountability is one of the biggest keys to success I have ever discovered. Practically anyone can write a goal down on a piece of paper, but how do you keep yourself on track? The power of an accountability partner is remarkable. Find someone whose life in some way captures your admiration and respect and you will be on your way. Engage them in conversation. Befriend them.

If you are still certain you have none, then by all means seek mentors and accountability partners. Ask if you must. Study their lives if you cannot. Connect with them.

In 1953, Sir Edmund Hillary became the first man to summit Mt. Everest. Please know there were over 400 team members or "accountability partners" with him on that expedition. He could not fail. Neither shall you.

Tenacity is both private and public.

My daughter loves our swing set.

I often wonder how long she would sit there swinging back and forth, smiling with every push, giggling here and there.

One day she surprised me as she refused my pushes and tried to imitate pumping her legs like her older sisters. She just couldn't get the rhythm right, though. She was making the swing jiggle a little, but she was not swinging. I admired her commitment, but I could see a meltdown about to erupt as her frustration increased.

I decided to help her out with a little push when she wasn't looking.

It can be a tough call at times, determining when to give a little push and when to let someone fail, and I'm not just talking about parenting anymore. There is much to be said for both, but there really needs to be balance.

I am so thankful to be surrounded by the positive encouragement of others that give me a little needed push to help me through a project. Sometimes that is all I need and I'm back on track, full steam ahead.

There are other times that I resist the advice and aid of others. I just want to try it on my own, risking a failed attempt if needed because there is no greater feeling than that of accomplishment. Sometimes I succeed. Most often I fail, but those failed attempts are such glorious glimpses of what soon will be if I keep trying.

It's important to know that not all pushes in life are helpful, and going it alone isn't always bad. The hard part, excuse me, the important part, is knowing when to accept and when to pass up assistance.

I'd be a fool to refuse all pushes.

I'd never grow, however, if I didn't try pumping my legs on my own regularly too.

Tenacity is about keeping after your goal with or without the help of others, and always finding a way. You don't get to skip practicing and jump right to mastery. No one is permitted to skip. We can however accelerate the process by reading books like this and gleaning tips from those who have traveled this path before, but the real key is developing tenacity and working toward your goal.

My dear friend Del talked me in to participating in some triathlons and endurance races. Boy were they a challenge! It's good to be challenged. It's good to do hard things. Del's tenacity was contagious. He made me want to work hard. Those endurance events truly translated into skills I use as a father, an educator, a coach, a writer and more. Always take on challenges; they build tenacity.

Tenacity is essential to leadership and I believe great leadership is impossible without it. Leaders are working toward progress and mastery.

A lot of people talk about life balance. They wish to balance work and fun and everything else they are trying to multitask in life, but tenacity isn't about balance. Tenacity is a medieval siege on a particular goal until it is conquered. Tenacity doesn't really allow much for balance. You know the work/life balance so many people dream about and desire. The truth is, the people that are really successful make sacrifices in order to achieve excellence. They commit. Tenacity is commitment to the vision. Not commitment at any price, but it does have a cost. Tenacity requires focus. As a wise man once said, "The man who chases two rabbits catches neither."

Leaders must fuel themselves with tenacity. This chapter has offered you much in harnessing tenacity and putting it to work. Only you can summon the leverage and passion needed to truly obtain the virtue of a tenacious leader. Get after it.

Commitment 3

The Third Leadership Commitment
I will lead with tenacity.

Beginning today, I will enjoy the thrill of a challenge and lead with tenacity. I understand that I will face setbacks. I now know that a setback is simply an opportunity for a comeback and greater success. I will embrace the notion of falling down and getting back up. I will approach challenges with passion and see failures as stepping stones of success. I know I am a work in progress and am proud to be in a beta format. I know the only way I can truly fail is to quit, and I will not quit. I will lead with tenacity.

Kelly Croy with American Astronaut and US Senator, John Glenn.

CHAPTER 7

Communication

A leader is someone who says, "Follow me," not just with their words, but with every action they take and every decision they make. Leaders are constantly communicating.

How do leaders communicate? They communicate with every step and word. They communicate with their body language, what they wear, and the activities they involve themselves with and what time they show up at the job. Leaders communicate with their first handshake to the last pat on the back, and every email, thank-you card, and phone call in between. Leaders are constantly communicating, even when they think they aren't.

Fair or not, we make opinions about people the moment we see them, and the same is true of leaders. A leader must be authentic and true to himself, but simultaneously cautious of the messages he or she is sending, both literally in a world of constant contact and communications, and symbolically through their appearances. Communication is important. Communication is essential to leadership. Be intentional with your communication.

If you want to maximize your influence as a leader you must learn to communicate effectively. You must write and speak well, but you must also learn and master *all* areas of communication.

A leader must let others know 'that they have your back', and 'together we will accomplish something big.' That's the message that influences people to want to follow and work with a leader.

How important is communication? Consider this, when something goes wrong and a complaint is filed within an organization or team, nine times out of ten the problem is one of communication. Furthermore, when a company or organization receives praise, the praise is better than 50% based on how well someone with that group communicated with someone outside. In short, communication is the source of most of our praise or most of our ridicule depending on how well we employ it.

Communication is either 95% of your problem or 95% of your success.

Master communication and you will become a great leader. All other talents and circumstances aside, if you can master communication you can lead well. You can make a problem look like an opportunity, and make an accomplishment feel like a championship, all in the story you deliver.

As a leader you must be clear to communicate what you expect from your team. If the people you are leading aren't clear about the goals, expectations, values, and results you want, how can they possibly follow and help you lead?

Leaders Make No Time for Gossip

Unfortunately, the majority of communication in our lives are complaints. A leader cannot be part of that. I make no room in my life for gossip. It's not a part of me nor my plan. Gossip is too small for me and so is complaining. I leapfrog both and go directly to work on repairing the problem. Instead of saying, "You know what's wrong?" work on "You know what would make this even better? Let me share my idea." When someone starts gossiping to you, you just have to interrupt with some positive comment. Do not subscribe to gossip or negativity. What you *don't* say is quite often as important as what you do say.

What you don't say, says the most about you.

"Those who gossip to you, gossip about you," is one of my favorite sayings. I remember it whenever anyone tries to entice me with a piece of gossip. I simply excuse myself. Usually, I say, "You'll have to excuse me. I don't know the whole story." And that's really the point, isn't it? We never really know the whole story. So, why do people automatically want to jump on the less flattering and negative side? I guess we know why, and that tells us much about their character.

Our world has never had a greater ability to communicate than we do today. We communicate through social networking, Facebook, Twitter, blogs, texts, emails, and even video chatting, and more. Still, we find gossip and ill-will, more often than not, at the center of communication. Sad. It seems our ability to communicate has unfortunately improved our ability to gossip.

"Gossip is as hard to un-spread as butter, " another of my favorite quotes and it's as accurate as it is funny. I see too many people's lives being harmed by gossip and rumoring. Our digital age is adding a permanence to these negative labels by creating a so-called digital footprint. When I was younger, when someone insulted you it could be forgotten over time, but today the internet keeps a digital record on everyone. It's more like a digital tattoo because it is so difficult to erase. Leaders must work to take care of their digital footprint and teach future generations to do the same.

Still, gossip is gossip no matter the form. We cannot allow a digital format to hold any more credence than word of mouth especially when its sole purpose is to harm. What we say and do behind others' backs says more about our own character than it does about the person we are talking about. Gossiping is poison for any organization or leader. There is nothing but trouble to be gained by continuing a rumor or talking poorly about someone.

Parents and educators teach their children not to gossip and organizational leaders must teach this as well. Furthermore, be innovative when tackling the problem of gossip and cliques. Encourage people to have lunch with different people to share ideas, mix up the special teams and groups from time to time, and eliminate cliques, not by demanding it, but by encouraging and supporting innovative diversity. Everyone has something to share and contribute. Help others see, value and communicate the values of others.

I encourage leaders to put an end to gossip in their personal lives and in their organization. Teach leadership that discourages all gossip and rumoring. Address it outright by letting your people know, "we don't talk like that here. That's not what we're about." Don't assume that it is "understood" that gossiping is against your organization's vision; make it clear. I recently read Dave Ramsey's excellent book, *EntreLeadership*, and in this book he explains that his organization goes as far as firing employees for gossip. He only gives them one warning. Wow! That is clear communication.

"A man or woman should always be remembered by their best qualities," another of my favorite quotes that I have shared more than once in this book. When something negative comes up about someone else I choose either to walk away or I mention one of their endearing qualities. You can use a positive phrase to let someone know you're uninterested in gossiping. For instance, when someone starts with a negative comment you can reply with some positive truth about the person, like, "Well, he sure knows a lot about marketing and gave a fantastic presentation last week." They'll get the idea.

We would think that adults would have a profound understanding about the dangers and improprieties of gossip, but that is sadly not the case. Gossiping about others is bullying, a waste of creative energy, a cause of inefficiency and trouble in the workplace, and a count against a leader's character.

Leaders make no room for gossip.

Leaders are Visible: The word *leader* comes from the concept of being out in the front. In fact, one of the oldest leadership principles is: Lead from the the front! As obvious as this principle is, it is also sadly, in fact, one of the most ignored.

Throughout history the leaders are those who led their men in battle from the front, exposing themselves to great danger in the process. Seeing their leader out in the front inspired soldiers to give their best, extinguish their fears, make sacrifices, and most importantly become leaders themselves. When one leader would fall, he would be remembered fondly, perhaps even as a legend, and another would rise up in his place.

It's not easy to be out in front. You need courage. You need confidence. Being out in front is the best communication you can ever deliver. **Be visible**.

You can lead from the front in many ways. One of the best is to simply keep in good communication with all of your people. Touch base with a quick email, in-person visit, phone call, or memo. Let them know you are backing them up and what results you are looking for them to provide. Make an appearance on their turf so they know that you know what's going on at every level. Let them know your expectations. In return, listen to them. Ask meaningful questions. Provide them with the tools they need. If you're not communicating, you're not leading.

When you are a leader there is no job beneath you! You can't look at a task and think that you are above doing it. As a leader you have to be willing to get your hands dirty. In fact, "willing" is not a strong enough word. You have to be <u>eager</u> to get your hands dirty! Make those tough jobs fun and rewarding for everyone. You can't do all the jobs, nor should you, but from time to time you need to show your people that you are eager to do a little of what they do to stay in touch and to understand the organization at all levels. You can't be expected to do someone else's job perfectly or even as well as they do it, but when you do it with a great attitude you show them you value what they do and give new meaning to it. That's leading.

I recently read about one of my favorite companies, Zappos, that when they hire someone in an administration position, they require that the person first work the customer service phones and packaging lines. I love this concept. I've also heard of top CEOs like Steve Jobs and others that would routinely answer a customer service email or even return a phone call to a customer. What leadership! What communication!

Leading from the Front

There is this mentality that whatever the boss says everyone will do. In reality, everyone mimics in some form what the boss **does**, not necessarily what he **says**. If the boss comes in early, everyone is a little more willing to do so. Same thing if the boss stays late, picks paper off the floor, and rewards people for their efforts. This is also true if the boss comes in late, goes home early, and ridicules. People do what their leaders do.

You need to know the names of the people with which you work. You need know your people's interests and dreams. You need to help them reach their goals and they will be willing to do whatever you ask of them. You also must be willing to do whatever *you* ask.

My friend, Matthew Kelly, authored a great business leadership book titled *The Dream Manager*. In his narrative, Matthew illustrates the importance of leaders getting to know and helping their employees obtain their dreams. Doing so, will inspire them to help fulfill the dream of the organization and create strong retention, loyalty, and a workflow second to none. I encourage you to add Matthew's book to your library.

Leaders are not holed up in some office or confined to one corner of the locker room. No, a leader is everywhere and talking with everyone.

He is visibly doing the small jobs as well as making the big decisions.

When I was in college I returned home one summer to work for a company that delivered heating fuel for farm houses. Sometimes those jobs were pretty dirty and exhausting. The owner of the company was a great guy. He was willing to do any job in the plant. I cannot even count the times he jumped in a truck with me to do a job. He didn't just sit there either. He got out and connected the hoses and talked with the families. What a leader!

•••

One of the greatest football teams I helped coach had a senior class with a dynamic group of leaders. We had four captains that year, but in reality we had about eight. No one had the attitude that they were better than anyone else. They let each other lead at different times.

We went on to the State Playoffs that year, but what I will always remember most is what a great group of leaders that senior class was. Typically the sophomores were responsible for putting away our practice dummies, but not that year. It became a game to the seniors to see who carried the dummies into the field house. Well, as you can imagine, that positive attitude became contagious. Soon everyone on the team wanted to carry the dummies. They actually raced and competed against each other as to who would get them. What was once the worst job on the team soon became a contest. Those seniors even made sprints fun. I remember them staying after practice to do extra sprints every night. Their leadership became contagious. That was a successful season on many levels. Leaders model what needs to be done to win. Leaders help build other leaders.

Leaders Serve

The word Samurai means to serve. Jesus instructed us to serve. Martin Luther King focused on service leadership. The greatest leaders in our time all saw their role in leadership as serving others. Service is the most powerful form of communication possible.

A great leader looks for ways to serve others. A great leader views her job as an opportunity to serve.

The one thing you must know about communication as a leader!

It is better to say something than nothing.

Leaders who do not communicate create more problems than leaders who communicate poorly. You want to communicate even if the message isn't popular, even if you know the message will not be well received.

It is your duty to communicate even bad news to your team and it will create more forward moving momentum than no message at all. Why is this so? In the absence of communication, people will create their own story of why things are happening. If your lack of communication is creating gaps, please know that people are going to fill those gaps with whatever information they choose, and quite often it is inaccurate gossip that will be more damaging to morale and the overall vision of the organization. In short, absence of communication is still communication, and it is the worst type of communication a leader can issue.

Remember, you are *always* communicating.

Become a Master Communicator

To lead is to inspire people to become their greatest self. To lead is to be able to draw out from people more than they knew they could offer. To lead is to inspire and motivate. Communication is the key that frees the greatness in others. It is your communication that will awaken the leader in others.

Leaders must be conscious and intentional about what they communicate.

*"Outstanding leaders go out of their way
to boost the self-esteem of their personnel.
If people believe in themselves,
it's amazing what they can accomplish."*
-Sam Walton

Master How You Communicate with Yourself

I read a wonderful book years ago on sport's psychology titled *Toughness Training for Sports* by James E. Loher. In this book I learned that the majority of our self-talk is negative. The author emphasizes that negative self-talk is damaging and that positive self-talk improves the success of Olympic athletes. This is huge, because we can change our self-talk and give ourselves a great advantage.

What we say to ourselves is far more damaging than any criticism from others. Be intentional about how you talk to yourself and about yourself.

Sometimes this negative self-talk is picked up by others. They hear us talk to ourselves. They hear the "I blew that one!", "I suck!", and the occasionally "I'm an idiot!". Some people are even posting their failures on social media sites.

You don't have to go around bragging all of the time, but why advertise failures? Turn that loss into a lesson and post what you learned. Work at making the majority of your self-talk positive.

The experts suggests replacing, "Crap! I always miss that shot!" with "Next time I'm going to nail that shot!"

You must learn to make positive statements about yourself and when talking to others and with yourself.

You might be surprised who is actually listening to the comments you think you are only making to yourself, and even if they aren't listening, our bodies do indeed project what we are saying. I can see "Crap! I always miss that shot!" on a person's face as easily as I can hear it.

Feed yourself doses of positive self-talk and begin to be amazed at your results. Talking positively and creating some default positive mantras have been a major source of productivity and success for me personally. I also attest that doing so has helped me to create a winning attitude. People will always choose to follow and spend time with someone positive over someone negative any day of the week.

Communication and Discipline: Discipline yourself and work at your self-talk. Make a challenge or game out of it. Positive self-talk will directly impact your dealing with others, your attitude, your tenacity, and most importantly how you think, especially when confronting a challenge.

Practice makes perfect! What you say while playing a game will later on impact what you say at the office or on the field. Identify some key phrases you know you make and shouldn't, as well as some situations in which you make them. It might sound easy, but it takes some focused effort and discipline.

Please know that when I am talking about self-talk, I am not just referring to what you say out loud. I also mean those little negative comments you make to yourself in your head. Those count just as much as what you say out loud. When you catch yourself feeding your mind junk, replace it with a positive thought and statement. It works!

You need to work on positive self-talk and eliminate negative self-talk entirely. Be your own public relations worker. Get the message out there that you are confident, successful, and have a winning attitude. You need to sound like a leader.

Mantras, Slogans, and Mottos

Positive self-talk is used by top executives, professionals in all walks of life, and Olympic sports athletes. We can use it too. Create a mantra, slogan, motto, or an inspiring phrase.

Corporations and clubs have slogans. You should too. Create some powerful words to get yourself in a state of leadership. Create some go-to phrases to help you get out of a rut.

The words we use matter, whether we are using them to describe others or ourselves. We need to communicate these meanings very carefully and intentionally. Write and recite your creed regularly. We become what we envision.

Journal

The greatest method I have found for mastering communication with myself, and one of the greatest lessons I have learned in life is keeping a journal. When I started keeping a journal, everything changed. Everything!

How many times does something need to be recommended to you before you try it? Well, for me, it was far too long. Time after time, teachers, coaches, mentors, friends, authors, speakers, and those I admired as 'successful people' had told me to start keeping a journal. My response was always, "Nah. It's not for me." Maybe you are saying the same thing to yourself now as you read this. Stop. Hear me. Keep a journal.

If you don't have time to keep a journal than you also must not have time to make more money, become a better person, a better leader, live healthier, and advance in all areas of your life, because that is what keeping a journal does! I have seen people spend hours a day on Facebook tell me that they don't have time to journal. Yeah right! I am a devoted husband, an involved father of four, active in my church, teach classes, volunteer, compete in triathlons, and somehow manage three successful businesses, write books, and I keep a journal. In fact, I think it is the key factor that enables me do all of these activities and do them well. Give it a try! Start a journal today.

What goes in a journal? That's easy. Everything. You know those telephone numbers and notes you write down on scrap sheets of paper and can't find when you need them? Journal. Trying to recall what you ran that 5k in last spring? Journal. Your journal is your brain on paper. The original laptop. Write down your accomplishments, setbacks, goals, dreams, magic moments, and anything and everything that is important to you. As famed speaker and author Tony Robbins states, "A life worth living is worth recording." This seems to have served him and the millions of lives he has impacted very well.

For the most part, journaling is daily, personal, and impromptu. It serves me. I am not writing for others although I do at times consider the legacy I am leaving behind for my family. I know they can advance by reading over the lessons I have experienced and worked through if at some later point they choose to when I'm gone, but I write for myself.

> *"Your role as a leader is even more important*
> *than you might imagine.*
> *You have the power to help people become winners."*
> **-Ken Blanchard**

You must be decisive.

Making decisions is what leaders do. The decisions you make must support the vision of the organization that you are leading. People aren't going to like some of the decisions you make. Your ability to communicate will serve you well when talking about past, present, and future decisions. Become a master of communication.

Many of the reactions you will receive regarding your decisions aren't necessarily about the decision itself, but how effectively **you** communicated it. Was it timely? Did people feel involved? Were you overly authoritative? Did you announce too soon, too late? Did you consider and prepare for blowback, questions, and alternatives?

While you cannot make everyone happy with what you communicate, and you shouldn't even try, you need to weigh and consider the impact of what you communicate, and keep everyone informed. If you can't let people in on announcement, explain how "not letting them in on everything" helps the organization. Let everyone know why the decision was made and how you expect the decision to support the vision of the organization.

The Power of Encouragement

Leaders communicate praise .

Compliments are free. You're not going to run out of them. It's not like you only have a finite number to handout. Look for the good that others do. Don't be waiting to pounce only when there are mistakes. Give praise. Praise is one of the best tools in a leader's communication mailbox.

Praise, recognition, and encouragement are the very best ways to communicate as a leader. These are positive methods to provide feedback, and truly they are what make leadership roles fun. Who doesn't enjoy presenting someone with an award, sending a positive email of thanks and appreciation, making a quick phone call thanking someone for their time, or writing a note telling someone how awesome they did on a project?

Sadly praise, recognition, and encouragement are under-used by leaders for a variety of misconceptions. So many leaders incorrectly believe praise will make them appear soft, weak, and less powerful. Wrong! Praise makes you influential! Find ways to provide sincere praise in timely fashions. Don't just do it because it's *that time of year*.

I am a firm believer that you get more with a carrot than you do with a whip. Use those carrots! Praise people when they take even the smallest step in the right direction. Although praise is free it must be sincere. Never give out undeserved praise.

Get to know the people on your team.

Touch base with a quick email, phone call, or memo. Let them know you are backing them up and what results you are looking for them to provide. Let them know your expectations. In return, listen to them. Ask meaningful questions. Provide them with the tools they need.

Even an unexpected but well-timed text can mark you as a leader and a person who cares. Send someone that congratulatory message. Be quick to encourage and praise.

A few years back I competed in the Hood to Coast Race from the top of Mt. Hood to the Pacific Coast with eight other runners. It is an event I will always remember. Epic in both location and challenge. The race is 200 miles of incredibly tough terrain, thousands of runners, and you have to be ready to run at any moment of the day. Minutes before the race was about begin I received a text from the head of a school for which I had been doing some consulting work. I must have mentioned the race at some point in our meetings. This authentic leader remembered me, remembered the event, located the time, and sent me some encouragement. Wow! What encouragement is was! How did he remember the start date let alone the time? I was enchanted. From that moment on I wanted to work for that leader! I couldn't wait to repay the kindness and honor. Well done.

Saying NO is Leading Too!

One of the hardest lessons I have learned about leadership is the importance of being able to say no. You cannot learn this lesson too early in life.

I think a lot of people believe by saying no to someone they have failed that person. Saying no to some makes them feel like a quitter, however, in truth, you are often taking a great step in leadership. Your 'no' to that particular request allows you to commit to something greater. Saying yes to everyone allows you to spend too little time on lots of things, rather than dedicating your time and talents to areas where you are passionate and can make a difference. If the greats of history had said yes to every request they too would have completed very little and would not have been remembered. Leadership requires a focus of energy, talent, and passion. Focus is guided quite often by saying, "No."

Think about it, with every yes you give, you are giving a piece of yourself away. Yes, you are giving away pieces of you. Give yourself away with thought and concern. Consider the investment of time and energy you are giving away. Helping a friend move is a wonderful thing, but unless you want to grow up and be a professional mover you certainly don't want to do that every weekend.

Understand and employ the value of a polite and firm, "no."

Quite often when I have to refuse a request I follow it with something I can do. Maybe I will say, "No, I am unable to help, but I will ask a few of our friends to see if anyone is available."

How Many Voices Do You Own?

You need a variety of voices to make a variety of impacts. As a leader you really do need to create an arsenal of speaking voices, so that when your tone changes people take notice.

I once had a young student teacher that became a wonderful teacher, but when he first arrived to my classroom he only had one voice. He used the same voice to lecture as he did to ask questions and even discipline. The students did not respond to his discipline or even his questions because they did not hear a change in his voice. Once he mastered several different voices his teaching went up a notch. Students sat up and took notice.

People need to know through physical communication and tone when you are being sarcastic, having fun, serious, upset, and the spectrum of emotions that a leader displays during a term.

Everyone works on their loud, authoritative voice, however, there are many times when a quiet, soft, but direct voice is even more powerful. When someone changes that volume and lowers their voice people really work to listen.

Work on alternating tone, volume, and style of your communications. There are four types of sentences: statements, commands/requests, questions, and exclamations. Learn to use them all.

Punctuality

There are twelve points to the Boy Scout Law and any leader would be wise to include them within their individual creed of leadership: trustworthy, loyal, helpful, friendly, courteous, kind, obedient, cheerful, thrifty, brave, clean, and reverent. There was a story circulating that if the Boy Scouts ever introduced a thirteenth law it would have been, A Scout is Punctual. I guess if you embody the first twelve you would have understood that being on time is important, and communicates what kind of leader you are.

Legendary Green Bay Packers' coach, Vince Lombardi led his team on what everyone described as Lombardi Time. Lombardi time was not the actual time. It wasn't even being prompt. Lombardi Time was always fifteen minutes early. The players and coaches loyal to him, his values, and dedication to excellence lived by Lombardi Time. His record speaks for itself.

I coached for Gary Quisno and I am so thankful for the experience and opportunity. He is a legendary high school coach. Gary also employed this rule of being early with his coaches and players. Graduating from Miami of Ohio he often referred to it as Miami Time, because they followed the same rule. His coaches, including myself, called it Quisno time. I believe some of the players started calling it Rocket Time after our mascot. You get the idea. Being early speaks volumes about you as a leader.

A wise man once told me, you are never on time; you are either early or late. Be early. I think being late says to everyone, "This is unimportant to me."

Your Appearance Matters

If there is one element of leadership that is questioned more than any other it is that of appearance. People just don't want to face the absolute truth that appearance matters. And it doesn't matter just a little bit it, it matters a lot.

Survey after survey from the business world, education, and those of sociologists around the globe will point out how first impressions, dress, and people's overall appearance and style impact people's ability to work, influence others and lead. I have read amazing statistics that a hiring decision is made within a matter of seconds based on the appearance of the candidate.

I knew a corporate executive who had literally hired hundreds of executive level positions in his career based almost entirely on the shoes the prospect wore. When I questioned this practice he smiled and said, "Well, I have yet to make a hiring decision that I have regretted." Whether we agree with this method or not, doesn't matter, the fact remains that much of what people decide about us comes from our appearance and first impressions, so we need to make the most of them. If we accept this as truth, and do not act on it, then we are limiting our leadership impact; your appearance matters to others.

Leadership has much to do with sacrifice. Just as we sacrifice our time for others, among other resources, we must also make sacrifices in our appearance. Being comfortable is important for me when I work, but it is not always paramount. Do you have to be comfortable to do your job well? No. Can you do your job well, sometimes even better, when you are uncomfortable? Yes. I never found my football helmet, nor any of my football equipment particularly comfortable, but it served me well and enhanced my playing. The clothing and equipment I use during triathlons is hardly comfortable, but it serves me. Leaders must dress in a way that communicates leadership. We make sacrifices in some areas to make gains in others.

One night, years ago, I was working out at the gym and on the way home I had a flat tire. I was wearing old workout clothes and I was drenched in sweat. I stopped and put on the little tiny spare and by the time I was done I looked even worse. I was dirty and disheveled. I stopped in at a convenient store to grab a soda and the grocery clerk looked at me like I was about to rob the place.

I asked him for the soda and he had to step inside a walk-in cooler to grab one for me. When he reappeared he looked at me with eyes that burned holes in me. I felt horribly uncomfortable. I took my money out to pay for the soda and he exploded with anger. He accused me of stealing a pack of cigarettes. I was in shock and humiliated. I don't smoke, never have, and I absolutely don't steal. The worker at the store actually had me open my coat and turn my pockets out.

I told the clerk he made a mistake. I told him to playback the security tape. I couldn't stand the thought of being accused of something so awful.

The clerk was absolutely wrong. He should have never accused me of something he had no evidence of doing. He should not have judged me. Plain and simple, the clerk was wrong. However, I looked the part. I'll never know why he accused me, but at that moment I could have been cast in a Hollywood movie as a shoplifter. I had the costume and my facial expressions from such a bad night must have made me fit the role. Sadly, people do make decisions about us based on our appearance. What is your appearance saying about you?

A big part of leadership is presence. My first employer had this power over me to make me stand an inch taller when he was around. I wanted him to see my best work. I wanted to be a part of every project he was implementing. His presence alone inspired me.

Creating a Powerful Impression: The good news is that much of appearance is within our ability to alter and redirect. No one is suggesting plastic surgery, but there are many simple factors that we can elevate to create a bigger impact.

1. **Your smile is the most important thing you wear.** (I suggest you wear a little more though just to be on the safe side.) Having a smile on your face warms the hearts of others. Other people start smiling. They start getting curious about what you're smiling about. Smiling makes you look confident. One of my favorite movie lines is from the movie *Elf* with Will Ferrell. Will's character, Buddy, one of Santa's elves, says, "Smiling is my favorite." I love it. It works.

2. **Proper hygiene is imperative.** No one wants to work for someone with body odor, bad breath, or looks like a slob. Work at being clean, tidy, and smelling nice. Carry around breath mints if needed. Work at it.

    I read Issac Walterson's biography on Steve Jobs. Walterson reported that Steve's hygiene was so horrible Atari, an early employer, he was moved to work nights by himself because no one wanted to be around him. Did Jobs become a great leader? Yes, in many ways. Still, he had many areas that he could have improved upon too. Leaders are always making adjustments to accomplish and influence more.

3. **Appropriate clothing.** You don't have to wear a tie or a power suit, but you do need to reflect on what your clothes are saying about you. Steve Jobs is known for his trademark black mock turtle neck, 501 jeans, and New Balance tennis shoes. He chose each piece to send a message. What are your clothes saying about you? What message do you want to send?

   I know some in-demand speakers and entertainers that actually hire consultants to choose and purchase their wardrobe for events and presentations. Is this a waste of money? To many yes, but for these speakers and entertainers it is as important as the helmet and jersey of a professional athlete. They know the message they want to send and they make an investment to reap the rewards. I am not suggesting you need a style consultant, but I am suggesting you give thought to what you wear.

4. **Work out.** You don't need to look like a body builder and probably shouldn't, but people can always identify and respect a person that works out. We respect those who have disciplined themselves with regular workouts. If they can motivate and lead themselves to a better future, they can probably motivate and lead others. It does wonders for their well-being and attitude as well.

   When someone works out regularly they have an aura of energy and health about them. Exercise improves their overall being and they just generally seem more vibrant and happy. Living longer is also a plus.

5. **Arrive early and prepared.** I've covered this earlier and I just wanted to emphasize it one more time, you are always communicating. Communicate that you want to do well and that you are working to make a difference. Arriving early says, "This is important to me."

I know some of this may be difficult to read and agree with, and I also know that it isn't always fair, however, our appearance really matters.

Be neat and organized: Even our handwriting and spelling are important. I once heard a story about a manager at Disney that cost his employer tens of thousands of dollars in just one day because of bad handwriting. Seriously!

During his first week as a manager of a live performance, he wrote so sloppily on a marker board the showtimes for his performers to work for a Disney Park performance that many of the performers showed up at the wrong time and the performance had to be cancelled, thus resulting in tens of thousand of dollars in losses for Disney. Needless to say, a valuable lesson was learned. The manager acknowledged that this was his fault, a weakness, and he worked at his handwriting. He learned a very powerful but costly lesson.

If you are not neat and organized it will cost you time or money, and sometimes both. Every *thing* should have a place, and every *place* should have its thing. Work at it.

Does spelling really matter? I once pointed out to a pharmacist the spelling error on her marker board of the word *February*. February is one of the most misspelled words in the English language. She left the "r" out, as some people mistakenly do, however, she tried to tell me, *the English teacher*, I was wrong. I instantly became concerned about her proofreading my prescription and was internally questioning the quality of her work on my medicine. If she overlooks something as obvious as what I found and wouldn't correct it, what was her ego also allowing her to overlook? I proceeded with caution.

On a trip south of the Ohio River I found myself in need of brake repair work on my car. I pulled up to a garage that I had spotted and to my horror saw the twenty foot long word "maintenance" spelled incorrectly. It was huge. They spelled it "maintnance". Ouch! An entire letter was missing. I wondered to myself about how carefully they would examine my brakes. What would be missing if I let them work on my car? I spoke to the owner and he told me it had been missing for several years and they just decided to let it go. What?!?

Well, I couldn't. With a napkin and an ink pen I offered several possible scenarios for a remedy. "This is what I'd do," I said handing the owner the napkin. The man, never looking at my sketch, said with a half-cocked face, "You need that car fixed or not?"

I had to draw my line somewhere, and it wasn't spelling, and surprisingly it wasn't even proofreading. I draw my line in the sand that once the mistake has been identified a remedy must begin. If someone points out something wrong, as a leader you need to address it. If the man had said he was embarrassed and considering to repaint the building at some point, I would have accepted it. I wish he had even acknowledged the mistake but said he couldn't afford a fix at this time. (Even a message on the building saying, "We repair cars 10X better than we spell." Anything!) I stand on the side of correcting mistakes in a timely fashion. If you stand on the other, we can be friendly, but we will not be working together.

I walked out on the pharmacist and found another. I used my free towing again to pull the car to another garage. Small things matter.

Writing and Communication

To become a good writer you must read, and of course read, and also read some more. To become a good writer you must also write, write, and of course write often. I cannot encourage you enough as a leader to read good books and write.

Listening

Communication is not just talking. Talking is only half of communication. Communication is also listening. Become a good listener. A wise man once said, "The less you talk, the more you are listened to." Work at listening to experts, colleagues, and those you lead. Everyone has something worthy to share.

> *"We have two ears and one mouth so we can listen twice as much as we speak."*
> **~Epictetus**

Six Things Those You Lead Need to Hear

People hear a lot of things during the course of a day. Each and every word makes a lasting impact. Employers, bosses, coaches, teachers, advisors, mentors and leaders in all areas of life must choose their words carefully. As a leader, we aren't always going to have the right words at the right time, but we always need to try.

Here are six things I think leaders need to say more often:

1. **Yes!** We want to help those we lead and send them on the right path. The word "No" is often set as default. I think people need to hear 'Yes' more often. You don't have to give in to every request, just quantify when those you lead can do something. "Can I order new software for our department?" Try, "Yes, but not today. When we can figure out which program is best suited for our needs and come up with a plan to fund the expense, we will order it for you."

2. **I make mistakes too!** People need to be reminded that everyone makes mistakes, and that failing is actually the pathway to success. Fail, fail, fail, fail, success! Apple and Google call their first attempts *Beta versions*. People need to know what to do when failure happens, not be told simply, *not to fail*. We want those we lead to accept responsibility, show leadership, and try new things.

3. **You can accomplish anything!** I use to think everyone heard this from their parents. By the end of my first year of teaching, I knew this wasn't true. This really was a special gift my parents gave me. I placed no limitations on my future. I dreamt big, and went after and achieved goals that really should have been unobtainable. Remind those you lead every day that they too are limitless despite any odds or any environment. Remind them they can accomplish anything. That's why you like working with them! That's what makes your organization great!

4. **How can I help you?** People need to understand that they can always ask for help, but also need to know that you, as a leader, aren't going to give them the answer or do the work for them. Leaders aren't simply the evaluator of someone else's work; leaders are a resource from which to seek help. In the age of Google, answers sometimes come too quickly. Let those you lead know you are willing to lend a hand when they get frustrated, but at the same time you're excited to see what they can do independently. Solutions don't always have to be immediate. Help them understand the process of discovery, questioning, learning, and reflection through collaboration. Help them become another leader within your organization.

5. **Thank you!** There are many positive ways to express this sentiment. Let those you lead hear you tell them they did a great job or that you like the way they said or did something. Do this, and you will give them the equivalent of a 20 hour energy drink for their confidence. Even better, brag on them to a third party. This is the biggest reward anyone can receive. A thank-you can arrive in different packages, and they are fun to open at any age. (And they're free, so give a lot of them.)

6. **You matter!** Can anyone ever hear this enough? Sometimes we need to tell those we lead that they matter and we value them.

Retention becomes a problem within an organization when people no longer feel they are making a contribution. Let those you lead know that they matter and how they can continue to make a meaningful contribution.

I've put my foot in my mouth plenty of times and had regrets about some of the comments I have made. My intentions were always to challenge others to become their best, but it didn't always come out the way I wanted. The art of communication is one we must continually practice and adjust. This list serves as a reminder to me to be quick to correct and find words of encouragement. What would you add? What do you believe those you lead need to hear?

What's your response time?

Communication is essential to leadership. To communicate well is to influence others into making a difference. Most leaders understand the importance of communication, and they spend a great deal of time on what they want to say and how they want to say it. Unfortunately, many emerging leaders do not understand that *when* they respond is as important as their message, and in some cases even more.

A leader must master response times.

The story of NASA's Apollo 13 mission is a highlight in history of how leadership emerges during times of trouble, and how great response time identifies leaders within an organization and in life. The story of the Apollo 13 Mission is full of heroes, but what I love most about it is how the men in mission control, not just the astronauts themselves, are proven to be heroes for responding timely. They emerged as leaders. Rockstar astronauts being rescued by control room nerds. What a powerful story!

In a world dominated with the ability to communicate quickly with smart phones, laptops, and social media, it is sad that so few do. Calls are not returned promptly. Thank you cards are never sent. Emails fill inboxes. Text messages hang in limbo. Assignments miss their due date.

What is the consequence of not responding timely?

Much.

You may not be leading a mission to safely return wayward astronauts from a mission gone wrong, but you really should respond to every message with a sincere level of diligence and importance.

Remember, you're not replying to a message, you're replying to a person.

How do you feel when you are forced to wait on hold, an email remains unanswered, a call unreturned? If you're like me you begin to question whether it was received, question the person on the other end, become frustrated or worse.

When questions go unanswered people fill in the gaps. People often assume the worst. Inaccurate information is spread, and negative impressions are formed. *Am I not important enough to merit a reply? Is my question less important than others?*

Some leaders mistakenly believe that to respond quickly is a sign of weakness: they're afraid it will show they don't have more important activities, and that others will judge them inferior for too quick of a response.

But what does a quick response mean to the person receiving it? It tells them, "Hey! I matter. I'm important." We like people that recognize us, spend time with us, and reach out to us. We admire them. We become enchanted. We want to do business with them. We want to help them. A quick response is endearing. It fosters loyalty. It matters.

I'm hoping that the leaders that dig these communication moats around their castles don't mistakingly believe they are protecting themselves or their organization by delaying their response. They're not. They are, in actuality, creating more problems, creating more work and damaging the positive image they worked so hard to establish.

The solution: **Respond timely**.

But I don't have time to respond to everyone. Wrong! You can. You can't afford to miss a single opportunity to connect. You will be surprised how little time it actually takes.

Great leaders, in all walks of life, master the timely response. They don't react. They don't shoot from the hip. They measure, weigh, and time their response accordingly to each situation. Please consider your communication habits and see if timeliness is an area you may wish to give some greater attention.

Master the Lost Art of Letter Writing: I have embraced the power of technology and social networking, but I have not been so foolish as to have abandoned the single most influential and personal form of communication available — letter writing.

It still amazes me that I can send my words to someone thousands of miles across the country in such a short amount of time, and make an impact in their life, and perhaps even mine. Letter writing is indeed a lost art, and one that leaders need to embrace and master.

Can't afford to give your hard working employee a raise? Reward them with hand-written praise. Even a post-it note with a couple of well chosen words hand-written will go further than your most skillfully worded email or text, because you've made it personal. You took time out of your day for them. You created something tactile.

Letter writing isn't just a skill, when it's done correctly it elevates itself to an art form. Its power is *increased* by the fact that so few others participate in its creation. Think about it. Nothing is more cherished in the mail than a hand-written card or a well-worded letter. People receive hundreds of impersonal emails a week, but perhaps only one personalized hand written letter. (If even that.) When they receive a letter from a real person it is special. They cherish it. They will stare at the envelope and wonder what is inside.

Write letters. Write thank-you cards. Send a note of congratulations. Leave someone a personalized message of appreciation.

Someone took the time to pen this note for me? How unique! No one else does that! How special! What a standout! Wow! You took the time to do this for me!?!

There are few things as exciting as seeing a personalized letter in your mail. Not a form letter or junk mail, but a real letter written by someone, just to you.

A Letter to Compliment: Corporations and organizations receive a lot of negative feedback. It is rare indeed when someone writes a letter to offer thanks or recognition. Sometimes they like to reward that. I actually received a phone call from the CEO of OGIO bags once because I wrote a letter telling them how awesome I thought their bags were. They loved it. I was invited to assist with the creation of a triathlon sports bag. The product finally went into production, and it all started with my letter.

To Thank & Congratulate: I am always mentioning my Moleskine journal in my posts because I know of its incredible value in my life. I always keep a couple of thank-you cards in the built-in folder in the back. I like being first to thank someone for their help or congratulate them on a success. I strive to be first and I strive to be memorable. Always write thank-you notes and send congratulation cards. It's never too late. There is never a bad time to send a get well or sympathy card. Be on top of this!

Postcards: The power of a written letter is that it is personal. When you remove that personal touch and create a form letter that you mail to a hundred or more people, it is now reduced to junk mail. People just don't have time for these. My postcards are a little different because on the reverse side I use my artwork as the picture and that, at least for some, makes it a keeper and more importantly a reader. It is also very easy to personalize a postcard with one sentence and your signature. "I am looking forward to meeting you at this conference! ~ Kelly" A powerful one liner. Keep it short. If you can have custom made postcards available then do it.

I recommend writing one letter to someone you admire. Ask nothing in return. Just let them know you exist and you appreciate what they do. Practice your craft well. One day a door will open, and you will be remembered.

In communicating, be sincere, be authentic. Say what you mean. Keep your word.

Sometimes we must write a critique of someone. Perhaps you need to evaluate someone. A true leader finds a way to word the communication in a manner that is accurate but inspires growth in the individual. Never pen words that will leave lasting harm or are vindictive. That just isn't leadership. Leaders build other leaders.

You need to read well written letters. Study them. Practice. Enjoy the process. Find ways to make personal letter writing a part of your leadership practice.

Virtual Leadership: Using Social Media.

Social media like Twitter, Facebook, and Instagram is not for everyone, but it is a great way to get your team organized and together. It is something to consider, especially now that most people use mobile devices and spend a lot of their time on these sites. If you want to engage people you have to go to the platform they are using.

I've heard conversations about who should really be "on" social media sites. Should leaders take part? Yes! Whole-heartedly, yes! If ever there is a place where people need to be held accountable, stand taller, and maintain high standards, it is within online social media sites like Twitter and Facebook. Why? First of all, that is where people are spending their time. I just read a report that stated the average American spends as much time online in these social networks as they do watching television. Both numbers are high. Second, for some strange reason, some people mistakingly believe that they can lower their guard while online. Nothing could be farther from the truth. In reality, more first impressions are being made by a couple of search engine results before you ever get a chance to email, call, or write. Yes, leaders should be online and they need to know what to do. It doesn't involve much time, there are shortcuts, and leaders simply cannot allow their online representation to be left up to chance or other people's posts.

Twitter: Twitter is an awesome resource for connecting, networking, and learning from some of the best leaders in the world. It's also great for engaging with your team. You can ask them questions and they respond! No kidding! I recommend this as the number one social network to be on, and it is incredibly easy to learn and use. Did I mention it is quite enjoyable too? I hope we connect on Twitter. I use HootSuite to schedule future posts and sometimes connect those with Facebook. I also use an app called TweetBot on my iPhone and Mac as my Twitter client, and I send posts I want to read later using an app called Pocket as a read-it-later client. I highly recommend Twitter.

Facebook: A great place to invite people to interact with you and the projects you wish to see completed. Another great place to ask for help and spread the word of upcoming events, and share information. This makes a great starter website. I have a personal page for my family and a Facebook Page, which is set for a business and different from a typical Facebook personal account, for my speaking and art. Set a time once each day to go through your Facebook messages and posts. I make a playlist of about three songs. When it's done, so am I. Next project. Don't spend your day on Facebook. Visit it once or twice a day.

Website: Having a web presence is important for any organization and leader. It could be as simple as a Facebook page. I recommend everyone at least purchasing their own domain name if possible. If 'your name.com is available, grab it. From there you can build a simplistic website and add to it throughout your life. I have even purchased the domain names of my wife and my children. Don't spend a lot of time tweaking it and getting everything perfect. What a time waster! Get something simple started. You can also make a great website for free using tools like WordPress.com or an app called Weebly. There are many options.

LinkedIn: LinkedIn is becoming more and more valuable to me as I make new connections. Try it.

Google search and alert: You should add a google alert to your name. When someone mentions you on the internet, Google will send you an email. It's very easy to set up an alert.

Blogging: What a great way to practice and improve as a leader! Pick a couple of leaders you admire and follow their blog, then start your own blog to share your thoughts on leadership and inspire others. Leave some comments on other blogs and reply back to some comments on your own. Don't live there. Posts should be around 500 words or less. Those blog posts add up and could become a book by the end of the year. Tag each post so that people can find you and connect with you. I use WordPress for my blog.

YouTube: Go ahead and use the camera on your laptop or iPhone and record a short video once a month for those you lead. This makes great practice for you and a wonderful resource for others. You will improve the quality with each recording. The videos should not be perfect. Don't even try. YouTube is a great place to archive how to perform jobs as a training tool for others. Saves a ton of time when someone new is hired. Your training videos are made by your best employees, showcasing their best work. Create some welcome videos. Have your people watch from anywhere. People love to watch short, fun, and helpful videos. I use my YouTube site to share videos of my speaking and art.

Emerging social sites: A word of caution, because there are so many emerging technologies, you can really lose a lot of time and productivity. It seems like a new social media site is popping up every month. Be cautious. If one seems interesting or has the recommendation of someone I admire, I sign-up for free and reserve my user name. I keep a distant eye on it and keep my focus on Twitter and Facebook.

Won't social media take a lot of time? No. Don't live there. Set a time of day and a timer to reply and comment to those who had the courtesy to leave you a message. Just a touch-and-go of thanks and a quick I-see-you will make a huge impact. You can personalize this down the road. I thank people for commenting and ask engaging questions. I enjoy it and it doesn't take much time. Again, don't live there.

My recommendations: Control your identity: Grab your domain name, and experiment with social media. If you are already there or find yourself investing too much time in it, back off. Social media can be a great place to work on leadership skills, but unmonitored, it can really infringe on time spent on more important projects or with family. Track your time. I use the timer on my iPhone and walk away when it goes off. I know exactly what I want to do next. Think BIG projects. Social media is not a project. Learn the shortcuts around these social media sites and how they can interact with each other. The three pieces I feel everyone needs immediately are: Twitter Account, Facebook Page, and a blog. You get all of those for free.

In summary, virtual leadership is indeed important, but we cannot allow it to infringe with our leadership roles, with our family, employment, and dreams. Use social media and online communities to enhance your real world experiences, not to replace them. How leaders use these social media tools defines the range of their impact. Everyone has something to share. Never use social media to harm or ridicule. Use it to inspire, update, and educate.

Communicating on the phone: Leaders must be able to make effective phone calls. It always surprises me how poor some people's phone skills are, but it shouldn't. No one really teaches people how to effectively use a phone. Without practice making calls, how can a person improve? The following will help you master your phone and better manage your time. The calls I am referring are business calls not personal. Business calls need to be short and effective. Like my email inbox, I want to keep my voicemail inbox at zero and calls-to-return to an absolute minimum.

Answering: I always answer, "Hi, this is Kelly Croy." It eliminates the other person asking if Kelly is available and me acknowledging I am Kelly and all of that nonsense, plus they immediately introduce themselves and state their purpose. I then thank them for calling, ask a couple of probing questions, tell them I am short of time, and will get back to them via email if that is acceptable to them. This eliminates future calls and frees up time. (This is also why I have multiple email addresses. You graduate to my personal email over time.)

Journal: I do not write notes on scrap pieces of paper, on the back of napkins, nor type them on the computer. If the phone number or message is important enough to be written down, it will be written down in my journal. Everything goes in the journal. Get and use a journal. Keep notes on phone calls in your journal.

Keep it short: Track the time you are on your phone. This can be done with a watch, a timer, and most cell phones have elapsed time of call on the phone. Set goals at the start of the call. Let the person on the other end know that you have somewhere to be, someone else to talk with, or something else to do. You can even gently remind the person on the other end how many minutes you have been on the phone if needed.

Twenty-four hour rule: If someone calls you and leaves a voicemail connect with them within twenty-four hours. It should be by phone if necessary, but if it is something that can be accomplished in an email, apologize for not being able to return the call in person, and stress you wanted them to have the information to them as quickly as possible.

Magic hour: Make all of your calls at the same time. This is called batched calling. Try to make your calls between 9:00 AM and 11:00 AM this is the magic time for making effective use of your calls. People will not pick-up near lunch hours, and they will not be helpful in the afternoon. I have invested a lot of research in my calls and these are my findings. Use them. If you cannot call between 9:00 AM and 11:00 AM, the second best window is 2:00 PM to 4:00 PM. Mondays and Fridays are not the best days to call, however, stick to the twenty-four hour rule, and any contact is better than none. Make that call.

Closing the call: Give them an action and a due date. I always end the call with whom is doing what when. For example, "John, it was great talking with you. I have a meeting in five minutes and I need to review some notes. I look forward to receiving your proposal by email before Wednesday of this week. I have noted it on my calendar. Thank you. Make your day great." End of call.

Speaker phone or headset: Using a speaker phone or headset is extremely useful because it frees you up to do other things. (Like getting your inbox to zero.) Dr. Randy Pausch taught me this great time-saver.

Voicemail: Use it. Let calls go to voicemail. Your voicemail system allows you to spend time with the people you love or to get your work done. You listen to the messages all at once and write them down in your journal collecting the numbers. Return the calls you need to within 24 hours. There are occasions where this should not happen, especially if you have arranged a time for someone to call you. Obviously emergency calls and personal calls from family are the exception. My iPhone allows me to rewind and forward the message to any spot easily with the touch of a finger, and to choose the message I want to play first. These are great, great features. I can rewind to a phone number, or skip to the most important message first. I always let messages at home go to voicemail so I can be with my family. I listen to them when I have the time, find out what is needed, record it in my journal, and plan my action response.

Your voice: Don't underestimate the importance of your phone voice. I am a speaker and people want to hear that I can communicate powerfully, effectively, and clearly. They also want to know what I sound like, and how I handle impromptu situations. The same will be true of any leader. Strive for clarity and energy when you speak. Make people excited to talk with you.

Video conference: Skype, FaceTime, Google Hangouts and other video conferencing software are becoming more predominate. Give this thought. I recommend a headset at certain times. Give thought to your background and what you are wearing. Have a backup plan, like a cell phone number in case the technology fails.

If you feel your phone skills are lacking, my advice is simple, practice. Make more calls and commit yourself to making an improvement with each call.

Be a leader in all of your correspondence. Have the courage to pick up the phone and make things happen. Leaders respond timely.

Email: Here is the email Rule: Get Your inbox to zero by the end of each day.
Here is how you do it:
- **Terminate Junk:** I delete junk mail and forwards with a vengeance. I don't read forwards or jokes. I am quick to delete. I file everything else in folders.
- **Unsubscribe:** Get off marketers' lists whenever possible. Take a second to click that unsubscribe button and it will free you of lots of junk and give you back lots of time. So many people fail to do this one simple task that helps them better manage their email.
- **Folders**: I keep folders titled: Newsletters, Speaking, Financial,

Orders, etc. that I feel I need. Keep your folder list to a minimum. You can search your folders for old messages, or your entire machine for the ones you need. I go into these folders often. I never, ever delete messages. Ever. Unless they are junk or marketing.

- **Read, Respond, File:** You read the email just once and then you either delete (which is practically a never), respond, and file, then move to the next, read, respond, file. Some emails don't require a response.
- **Put the Ball in Their Court:** I respond in such a way that the sender needs to respond next. I don't worry about the email anymore. I responded, gave them an action to get back to me when "X" is completed, and I filed it. These actions usually include a date that I need a response by, and a thank you, but you need to give them an action to get back to you.
- **Take Action:** If the email is asking you to do something, do it. If you cannot do it immediately respond immediately to the person and tell them approximately when you can, then add it to your calendar with an alarm and put it on the to-do list. I often respond with, "I received your message regarding a commissioned art piece. I have several requests ahead of you. I am adding you to my inquiry list. To remain on the list, please mail a 25% deposit... I will email you once the deposit is received and an approximate date of completion." If you are able to delegate it to another, do so, and respond telling them why you delegated, and then copy it to that person. Request a notice from both that the arrangement is acceptable. If the email does not require action, file it.
- **Spontaneous Touch & Go:** Isn't it great when you get a "Just thinking of you message?" I send these out immediately if I see a friend has met an accomplishment or if I am indeed just

thinking of them. Why? Because I sincerely like doing it, and I would like the same in return. Always be first to compliment, congratulate, and thank.

- **Accounts:** This one is up to you, but it works great for me. I keep three email accounts, but all are accessible from any device, anywhere, and synced so when a message is deleted or filed on one device it is deleted or filed on all. I keep one email address for my family and friends, one for my business, and one for signing-up for new ventures.

- **Optimize Email Organization Times:** I complete 95% of my email management from my iPhone on the go. I delete and file in the checkout line at the grocery store, when someone else is driving, and whenever I have a moment to spare. I have a folder of attachments of frequently asked questions (most are about my speaking engagements) that I use with short personalization. This really speeds replies because it is a simple copy and paste.

Even more importantly, schedule times that you do **not** check email. Complete large batch email sessions at one time. Try to look at your inbox just a couple times a day for management. You do not need to keep checking! Setup "NO" email times and locations and follow them. Your daughter's soccer game is a GREAT example of where NOT to get the email down to zero. Do NOT make responding to your inbox your job. Move quickly and get that inbox to zero. If you find email taking more time than you want, just use your timer on your phone or microwave, or play one song in iTunes, and get after it. When the song or timer goes off, stop. This is batch email processing. Keep emails short!

You can get your inbox to zero easily each and every day. Remember you are not responding to an email, you are responding to a person. If you don't get to zero, at least get it close. Don't make email your priority, but don't let emails slow you down. Email is a powerful tool for a leader.

My friend and mentor, Michael Hyatt, has written a great book titled *Get Noticed* that can really help a leader to better understand and implement social media. You should pick up a copy and visit Michael's website at www.MichaelHyatt.com.

Leaders Must be Visible

Work the Room: If you want a fast way to increase your influence as a leader, learn to work a room. One of the most powerful ways to connect and influence is to acknowledge people whenever you see them. Never pass up an employee or team member without a handshake and a word of encouragement.

Some people find this a little uncomfortable at first, but it just takes a little practice. I love meeting new people and reconnecting with others. Even if I didn't, I would still understand the importance and responsibility of a leader connecting with people.

When you enter a room you smile and shake hands. Share a few sentences with that person. Make eye contact. Move on to the next person. Make it your job to connect with everyone if possible.

If someone wants a conference or to have a major discussion, tell them to contact you on your personal email or schedule a call. Remind them you want to visit with everyone in the room. Assure them that once you hear from them you will follow-up. Keep your word. Thank them. Move on.

Learn People's Names: The president of my college was an amazing man. His name was Dr. Debois Freed. He was a graduate of West Point. Besides being incredibly wise and kind, he had one of the most amazing talents for knowing people's names. It was uncanny.

Ohio Northern University was a small college, but to learn everyone's name would still be an amazing undertaking. Dr. Freed would hand us fruit during exam week. We would stand in line and he would hand us some fruit calling us each by name. There was no assistant, there was not ear piece, there was no list. He did it by memory.

The result was amazing. We felt like a somebody! The president of our college knew our name! Wow!

Years after graduating, a friend of mine attended an alumni celebration and she told me Dr. Freed still remembered her name. Amazing.

The same will be true for those you lead when you learn and use their names. Don't let it stop there. Learn about a hobby they have, a project they are working on, the names of their children. Sincerely take an interest in the lives of those you work alongside and they will follow you with admiration and loyalty.

How to Introduce Someone: There are three types of introductions: good, bad, and memorable. In order to create a memorable introduction you must complete six important steps:

1. Say their name and often. Say their whole name clearly and slowly.
2. Put your hand on the shoulder of the person you are talking about.
3. Look into the eyes of the person you are speaking to, not about.
4. State how you know the person.
5. State something they do incredibly well professionally.
6. State something else about the person that is positive and engaging.

Then you do it for the other person.

The result is amazing. The two will learn each other's name, have some admiration for each other, realize how they can network, and have something to talk about. Also, each will admire you for speaking so highly of them. That's a memorable introduction.

Ideally your introduction looks like you are showcasing a dear friend and presenting them to someone else to have in their life. The hand on the shoulder, the eye contact, the three statements you make about the person, all combine into a memorable introduction. You can now walk away and be assured the two will be able continue on without you.

Example: "Tom, this is my good friend Mark. Mark and I met when I worked in Watertown, Massachusetts at Perkins School for the Blind. Mark is an amazing physical therapist. He works with physically challenged children and helps them better engage with their world. Amazing guy. Mark plays a guitar pretty well too."

Also note in the example how many times I said "Mark" so that the listener would 'get' the name. Once is never enough.

If you are the person being introduced you extend your hand and say something like, "A pleasure to meet you, Tom." Yes, you say their name. Look them in the eye and smile.

One of my speaker friends, Mark Scharenbroich, has written a great book about recognizing others and acknowledging them in casual conversation. The book and method are both titled *Nice Bike!* He is an amazing speaker and great guy.

More Valuable Than Gold: At some point you will need to make a decision that is going to be unpopular. First, make certain you aren't making it for personal reasons and gains. Make sure your decision reflects the vision of the organization you lead and the character traits you have worked hard to best represent. Make sure your decision has been guided by wisdom, and having a mentor to bounce it off is also a good idea. If you have met all of these criteria, I doubt the decision will be met with much criticism, but if it does your communication skills will be of more value than a king's ransom. You will explain how the decision best serves all involved. Leaders who say nothing, feed the confusion and derail progress. It is always better to say something than nothing.

Make Your Communication Personal: Whenever you can avoid sending out a generic mass email or photocopy you move up a notch with your communication leadership skills. Whenever you don't hold the meeting that could be covered in an email or some other notice, you grow as a powerful leadership communicator. Making personal connections whenever possible is the greatest communication skill a leader can implement. I realize mass emails and meetings must happen and they are easy, but make them count, don't make them a staple of your leadership style. Be personal whenever possible while communicating and value everyone's time. Less really is more.

What's Most Important? The most important communication a leader makes is that of the vision of the organization you are leading. Communicate the vision. Communicate the vision to those you lead and to the public. The second most important communication a leader makes is communicating to those you lead how they help to fulfill the vision. You, as the leader, are responsible for making sure those you lead understand how they are to help fulfill the vision and whether they are doing it effectively. The third most important communication, is how a leader authentically communicates to himself. This communication needs to positive but realistic. This communication also needs to focus on what needs to stop, start, and continue.

You are always communicating. Always! I really can't emphasize this enough. I know a leader that walks into a room, says very little to anyone if anything at all. What he doesn't realize is that his silence says volumes to everyone. If they didn't see him, it sends a message. If they saw him and he didn't say anything to them, it sends a message.

Leadership is most often described as having the ability to influence others. It's no surprise that most of our influence stems from how we communicate. Most problems come from poor communication, and most success from great communication. Seize the power of communication in leadership. Master how you communicate and you will master how you lead.

You have many tools in your communication toolbox to help you lead. Keep adding to that communication toolbox.

Commitment 4

The Fourth Leadership Commitment
I will consistently work at becoming a powerful communicator.

I will work from this point forward to master my ability to communicate. I fully understand the tight relationship between leading and communicating. I realize I am always communicating and will be more self-aware of the messages I am broadcasting as a leader.

Kelly Croy with legendary Notre Dame Football Coach and sports commentator, Lou Holtz.

CHAPTER 8

Vision

Promote a vision that others willfully wish to fulfill.

Vision is the entire purpose of Leadership. It's the dog in a corn dog, the noodles in spaghetti, and the music at a dance. Without vision, a leader is nothing more than someone moving around making noise. The vision is the purpose of an organization. It's the mission, or the direction in which the organization wants to move toward.

Know this, an organization's vision must be clear to everyone involved, and that is the job of a leader. A leader must work toward obtaining this incredible ability to get everyone to enthusiastically work toward this common vision. In times of setback, defeat, and even failure, a true leader rallies everyone toward the vision once again. In times of success and celebration, the leader gets everyone to recommit and further advance the vision.

So many organizations just get vision wrong! They play this word game with members of the organization and try to make them feel like each is helping to create a mission statement, but they're not. In reality, each member opposes the process and doesn't feel part of the vision of the organization at all. Each person needs to see their role in a simple, clear vision. They must feel they are contributing, not just be told that they are, and certainly not hanging up a poster that says they are. They must feel it. The vision must be felt by each person. That is the job of the leader.

A vision statement, mission statement, or whatever you wish to call it, actually is important, but it needs to be simple and meaningful. A vision statement is about improvement. A vision is not just a goal, or depiction of what could be; it is an opportunity, a challenge, a plea to your future self.

To lead yourself, you need to be able to see a better version of you. In order to lead your organization you need to be able to see an improved version of your organization. The better you can picture it, the better you will be at leading toward that goal. That's why it's called a vision. You must see it! Everyone must see it.

The vision must be written down, reflected upon and broken into goals. These goals need deadlines, however, the vision needs to be big enough so that it cannot be measured in terms of obtainment.

A vision needs to be ongoing. If the vision actually is met and obtained the purpose of the organization has been completed, and therefore the organization is no longer needed. If the vision is fully met then a leader is no longer needed, just a manager at the most. Leaders take themselves and organizations to places they currently are not at, or perhaps may never have been before and that means there is going to be change. Vision is about change.

Create a Culture of Engagement

People need to hear the words, "We need you." If you want an engaged work force, they need to know they are valued!

Write a note. Make a call. Announce it in your newsletter.

Let your employees, family members, and teammates know you need them, and that they add value on a regular basis. Don't wait until the yearly evaluation or exit interviews, or when there's a problem to let them know. Let them know what their purpose is on your team regularly, whether it's business, sports, or home.

People Matter

Everyone in your organization needs to be reminded of how they play a part. Remind them that they are a part of the team and a part of the vision.

As highlighted in an earlier chapter, communication is crucial and one the most important messages you can deliver is reminding each member how they contribute to the overall vision and success. A great leader has acquired the ability to share the vision with everyone and passionately explain how each member plays a part. They engage the members, show them their role, and their part in the journey.

Never let anyone feel like they aren't a part of the big picture. Each member should personalize the organization's vision with a specific emphasis on their role. You should be able to state how each person contributes and each member should as well.

How to Improve Retention

Many companies and programs struggle with retention. It's a costly problem for organizations because they have to retrain and cover the absence. This is true in sports programs, corporations, families, and everywhere people work together for a common goal. The number one reason people leave is because they no longer feel they have anything to contribute, and that is primarily the fault of the leader. Take the time to review regularly with your team their role, responsibilities, and contributions. This vital step will eliminate most problems before they arise.

Most retention problems don't occur because of salaries, playing time, bonuses, or awards. People leave and become disengaged because they no longer feel they matter. They feel unwanted, unneeded, and that they have no purpose. Everyone wants to have a purpose.

Problems with retention aren't just financial concerns, it also speaks volumes about your organization's culture and your leadership. The retention problem grows and soon becomes a marketing problem, customer service problem, and more.

People wonder: *Why do people keep leaving? Why can't they keep people? Do I want to be part of something where you feel undervalued and unappreciated?* No. No one does.

Good leaders communicate a purpose to each member regularly. They connect the member to the vision, and the vision to the member. Making the connection doesn't have to be all praise either. Sometimes the leader must show the person's value by correcting how they **aren't** contributing to the vision fully. Express the words, "We need you. You are an important part of our vision. You matter." Then tell them what they need to accomplish. Be clear.

If a member needs redirection toward the vision, then that should become part of the regular informal evaluation process and formal evaluation process. You can identify an area for improvement in a positive way.

We have to do what our boss says, yet we want to do what the leader says. Big difference. Leaders are able to make everyone stand an inch taller, work a little harder, and on occasion, do what shouldn't even be possible. I've seen it happen, and it's amazing. Maybe you have seen it too. We remember these leaders, and we remember they didn't accomplish it through inciting fear. People wanted to give to the bigger vision; they wanted to help the leader.

As the leader you need to communicate the *sentiment* : *As the leader, I acknowledge the contribution you make to our overall vision, and it is important.* Or even more simply: *What you do matters. You matter.* This needs to be done with every person on the team. From the designer of the product to the person that delivers it.

Once that person feels that sentiment, not just hear it, you can help them grow in ways to make an even stronger contribution to what your organization is all about.

Most often a leader acquires a vision created by those that came before him. A leader must develop ownership of that vision and make it his own. Some CEOs or managers fail to succeed not because they aren't talented, they are, but because they were never truly able to own the vision of the organization to which they pledged their service. You must agree with the vision of the organization of which you will lead, own it with passion, and personalize it with your own flair.

> *"A leader has the vision and conviction that a*
> *dream can be achieved.*
> *He inspires the power and energy to get it done."*
> **~Ralph Lauren**

A leader must be able to influence others toward a common vision. This vision is either one that is created by the leader himself, or a vision that has been established by the organization. If the leader is the captain of the ship, then clearly the vision is both the ship's destination, and mission. Ships do not set sail without destinations and missions and neither should a leader.

On rare occasions leaders have the opportunity to create a new vision. If you do not have a vision yet, adopt one you admire until you can construct your own. Sometimes we use the vision of others as models for our own. Regardless whether your organization's vision is decades old or relatively new, one you created, or one passed down, the vision must be adopted and personalized by all on the team. Each must align their role of how they will help make it happen.

The Vision Must:

1. Be incredibly short! In one sentence be able to state the vision.
2. Include everyone together to achieve it, not separate individuals.
3. Challenge people to do their best work and become their best!
4. Be shared regularly.
5. Inspire enthusiasm and excitement. You are part of something bigger.
6. Encourage participation beyond normal expectations.
7. Be understood by all.

Vision = Navigation System

A vision is the GPS navigation system for leaders. Like the guidance system in any vehicle, it doesn't drive the vehicle, it informs the driver which direction to follow and its aim is to keep the driver on track. When the driver changes course the GPS helps them get back. This is what a vision is to a leader! A vision provides the feedback needed to lead.

Whatever vision you are leading your organization toward, know that it is bigger than any embarrassment. All leaders encounter failure, but what separates great successful leaders apart from unsuccessful leaders, and it sounds a bit cliche', is that successful leaders work toward the vision until it arrives. You will fail more times than you succeed, but you will remember success far longer than you will a setback.

In 1989 I worked part-time at the famed Perkins School for the Blind in Watertown, Massachusetts. Perkins is known globally for the incredible level of education they provide for children with visual and auditory challenges. They help students confront the physical and mental demands of the world and they teach them how to live richer and more independent lives. I have the highest regard for Perkins

School for the Blind. It was quite simply one of the most influential experiences in my life.

Working as a program aide at Perkins was an experience that impacted my life greatly and helped shape who I am today. The vision for the school was originated in the early 1800's by a man named Dr. John Fischer while in medical school. Fischer had an epiphany about starting a school to assist the visually impaired and the more he thought about the idea, the greater his passion grew. Returning home to the Boston area he began summoning other leaders to help him refine the vision and start such a school. Again and again, Dr. Fischer shared his vision and slowly the idea became a reality. He implemented his vision at first in small ways by converting the empty rooms of his father's home. He didn't wait until he could build the elaborate campus which Perkins has today. He just began.

> *"Do what you can, with what you have, where you are."*
> **—Theodore Roosevelt**

Fischer had a vision of a school that could better the lives of the deaf and blind, and he communicated that idea to other influential leaders, and pursued his dream with tenacity until it became a reality. He knew that his own vast knowledge was still not enough and he sought and acquired the wisdom of others. His can-do attitude and his authenticity as both a scholar of medicine and philanthropist brought about the wonderful Perkins School for the Blind. His impact, however, did not stop there.

The school later trained a great teacher named Anne Sullivan who forever impacted the world with her passion for teaching and commitment to help others. The school had already assisted students who were both deaf and blind, but Anne took on a challenge of her own, an uncooperative student named Helen Keller. Had she just helped Helen live an independent life, her purpose and that of the school's would have been validated, but Hellen Keller's life was more than independence. Helen's accomplishments impacted millions through her lecture series, twelve published books, and her work as a political activist. She has become a household name, and her impact lives on long after her death.

With each new success Perkins continues to broaden its vision and grow. The core remains the same but their reach grows and adapts with each generation. Allow your vision to grow and adapt while keeping its core principles intact.

Broaden Your Vision: The work we complete as leaders really has no limitations. We will never know the depth of the impact we have on others. We will never know the number of individuals our work has influenced. We will never know how we influence future generations. Just know that it does. The vision you help fulfill will continue to impact long after you are gone. Serve your vision well.

> **"Give me your tired your poor,**
> **your huddled masses yearning to breathe free.**
> **The wretched refuse of your teeming shore.**
> Send these the homeless, the tempest tossed to me.
> **I lift my lamp beside the golden door!"**

By Emma Lazarus, from The New Colussus

These powerful words are inscribed on the pedestal on which the Statue of Liberty rests. As our country begins yet another new chapter, these words are a refreshing reminder of the power and responsibility of being an American. They also serve as a reminder to give thanks, even in times of hardship and personal challenge, for the opportunities that truly, only America can offer.

The Statue of Liberty holds a special place in my heart as I am sure it does for all Americans. My grandmother and grandfather immigrated here from Ireland. I grew up listening to my grandmother share stories about being aboard a ship and seeing the Statue of Liberty for the first time. My grandmother immigrated here because of the American Dream. Being the youngest of a potato farming family during times of great hardship, she was in some way a part of that "wretched refuse" and the journey here definitely made her "tempest-tossed." She was by all means looking for opportunities.

These wise words penned by Emma Lazarus are indeed inscribed on the Statue of Liberty's pedestal. While we all know that Lady Liberty was a gift from France, many do not know how the large pedestal on which the statue rests was constructed by New Yorkers.

Residents of Manhattan were asked to donate ten cents each to help fund the construction of the pedestal. The pedestal would provide a base for the statue to rest and elevate it so it could be seen from great distances. The work would take months to complete and was very expensive. Nearly all residents were eager to donate to this worthwhile cause, but there were of course a few who saw this endeavor as a waste of time and money.

Arthur Miller wrote a story of one such man who complained about the fundraising for the pedestal, and the story is a favorite of mine to share in highlighting the importance of leadership. Like an Ebenezer Scrooge, the man in Miller's story refused to donate and he found fault with everyone who gave money to the project or helped to organize the fundraiser.

It is important to note that no one had seen the Statue of Liberty yet. It was in a warehouse in pieces stored in crates. They had read about it and seen drawings and pictures, but it had not yet been assembled in the United States. Everyone was anxious to donate and see this amazing work of art, and beacon of freedom assembled. It was quite difficult, however, for Miller's stingy character to visualize the majesty of this ten-story statue and so he never donated to the fund for the pedestal, not one dime.

Some time after the construction of the pedestal and the assembling of the statue, the man's grandson begged the old man to go and see the statue. He tried to refuse, but couldn't. Upon arriving at Liberty Island in the New York Harbor, the man was in complete awe of Lady Liberty. He was literally speechless. The statue's size and grandeur, as well as the sense of freedom it conveyed completely overwhelmed him. Eventually the man and his grandson ascended to the top of the observatory inside Lady Liberty's crown. With a tear of shame running down his cheek, the man took a silver dollar from his pocket and jammed it into a small opening he discovered. At last, he finally made his contribution. He could not stand knowing that he was not part of something so wonderful.

Do not be like this man in Arthur Miller's wonderful story, *Grandpa and the Statue*. The old man lacked vision; he was unable to visualize what the Statue of Liberty would mean.

Get Out of the *NOW*: Answer the call to lead and make a difference in the lives of others. Allow your vision to expand beyond the ever growing demands of *now*. We must train ourselves to think *longer*. Vision is thinking about what actions need to happen over time to get the desired result.

Our life is brief, but the contributions we make and the roles of leadership we choose are timeless. Looking into the future helps us to make better decisions. We are no longer choosing what is best for the moment, but rather, what is best long term. What will have the greater impact, growth, and meaning? These are the choices of a leader.

Jesus envisioned a new kingdom. Martin Luther King envisioned a society free of prejudice and racial barriers. Your vision has to be forward looking. Your vision should be grand.

An inspiring vision will help you make extraordinary choices. Your vision should serve every decision you make as a leader. Know your vision well. Reflect on it often. Engage others whose opinions you respect in a discussion on your vision from time to time. Keep the vision timely and adjust it to the challenges of the times while keeping the principles aligned.

"Cowards and critics don't have vision, only anti-vision. Instead of taking risks they criticize those who do."
~John Bryson

The Organization's Vision: Some organizations call this their mission statement, speakers and writers may call this their message. It doesn't matter what you label the vision, just as long as you know the vision, clarify it for your team members, reference it daily, and measure your outcomes to it. Some organizations create slogans or advertisements that reflect their vision to keep it short and memorable.

Vision

1. **Write your vision down. Make the vision visible to you and others.**
2. **Clarify it for yourself and the members of your team.**
3. **Read it aloud personally at least twice a day.**
4. **Reference it regularly in meetings, correspondence, and conversation.**
5. **Measure your progress to this vision.**
6. **Reward team members for contributions that further the vision.**

Vision is a point of focus that a leader uses to guide and lead. It is the reference point by which the leader uses to evaluate himself, the organization he is leading, and those with which he is working. The vision is the master to which the leader serves.

Leaders who lack vision should never be given authority over visionaries. The best leaders are visionaries that work hard.

"A leader is one who sees more than others see, who sees farther than others see, and who sees before others see."
- Leroy Eimes

A real danger when using the word vision is that it sounds just too far off into the future. It may sound as if it is not something that can be worked on in the here and now. So, the first job of a leader is to connect that vision to everyone involved and make it part of the day to day work. Visions are broken down into goals. Sports teams are able to do this rather well. Coaches connect even the smallest movement in a drill to a championship title. It works.

Leaders are connectors between the vision and the team. They remind people of the vision and what needs to be done in times of distraction and setbacks. The leader models what needs to be done in the moment to achieve the future result. Leaders make the vision seem worthy of being sought after and obtainable. The leader always has the vision in sight.

"The very essence of leadership is that you have to have a vision. It's got to be a vision you articulate clearly and forcefully on every occasion."
~Theodore Hesburgh

When you need to create a vision, first make sure that there isn't one that already exists. Most often, organizations already have a vision, but it just hasn't been written down yet. If you must create one, simply ask this question:

Ideally, what single lasting impact do you want this organization to accomplish?

A business cannot make earning a billion dollars their vision. Nope. That might be a goal, or a task, but not a vision. The vision is what your business strives to offer the public; the money you receive is separated from it. If you do your vision well, the latter will follow. If earning the billion were truly the vision then anything that earned money would work within the day to day operation of the organization, and that simply isn't what your organization is about. Examine the product or service you wish to deliver. That should be the focus of the vision. The rewards for following the vision will arrive as the vision is brought to reality.

In sports the vision is simple. We keep a win-loss record. Obviously we want more wins than losses. Ideally we are always seeking that league championship, the conference championship, and so forth, but we never do this by sacrificing ideals, rules, and sportsmanship. While winning is important it is not the only area of focus. So, winning the title is our number one goal, but our vision is to play our best each and every down.

> *"There's nothing more demoralizing than a leader who can't clearly articulate why we're doing what we're doing."*
> **~James Kouzes and Barry Posner**

What makes a great leader is that he is able to identify how each member contributes to the overall vision and influences them to give freely of their talents and resources to make the vision a reality. The leader is great because he helps each member in the organization see what can happen if they fully participate. The leader sees *what can be.*

Using Vision as an Evaluation. Too often organizations evaluate team members in areas that just simply don't translate into how well they are contributing to helping the organization realize their vision. Instead they evaluate them on the "to-dos" of the day to day flow that quite often distracts people from really working on the vision. Leaders should use the vision as the ultimate measure.

In order to know where you are going, you need to know where you are. That is true for the leader and each member of the organization. Have members evaluate themselves in regards to the overall vision of the organization. See if they understand how they contribute, what they are doing well, and where they need to improve. Help them in these areas. If they are lost, show them the way. A leader needs to recognize what others need.

A very simple evaluation method is to ask those you lead each week how they feel they contributed to the vision of the organization. Ask them to share a high and a low point during the week. Ask them if they found any tricks or tips to help them repeat the high points, and ask them if they found a solution to the low points. Some organizations are realizing the necessity of having employees create a short, weekly, internal blog posts about key solutions to their organization's challenges so they can share them with current and future co-workers.

Once again I lean on the most import quality of a leader as highlighted in chapter one, attitude. Your attitude will influence your vision more than anything. A great attitude will ensure a great vision and a sour attitude will build a weak vision. What we feed grows and what we starve dies. Keep your attitude congruent with your vision.

Here is The Walt Disney Corporation's mission statement:

"The mission of The Walt Disney Company is to be one of the world's leading producers and providers of entertainment and information. Using our portfolio of brands to differentiate our content, services and consumer products, we seek to develop the most creative, innovative and profitable entertainment experiences and related products in the world."

This is a great mission statement and vision for a company, but you don't fully appreciate this vision until you watch a Disney movie, visit one of the amazing parks, see one of their shows, and even meet one of their workers. Each experience delivers this mission statement in the quality of their work. The Disney mission statement isn't written somewhere and put on a shelf it is embodied in all they do. It is understood by all.

The goals The Walt Disney Corporation set in their five year, three year, one year, monthly and even daily plans will be very specific, but will support this mission statement. The goals are the "how will we do this" of the mission statement.

Vision works hand in hand with communication. A leader must communicate the vision to all involved and there are many ways to accomplish this. A leader's job is to bring everyone into the common vision and help them contribute to its success. A leader needs to let them know they are crucial to the outcome, that each person has purpose.

> *"If you are working on something exciting that you really care about, you don't have to be pushed. The vision pulls you."*
> **~Steve Jobs**

Vision Boards: Some leaders have been successful creating vision boards. A vision board is just what is sounds like. It is a collage of visual images that represent your written vision. It is great for starting discussions, expanding the vision, realizing the vision, and beginning a goal setting workshop. Ask team members to bring in a visual representation of how they interpret the vision. Post it on the board and discuss.

Sometimes other images are helpful. Having a blueprint to a future building project made or an artist's representation of that building will help fulfill it. Every day people will walk by that image and think, "How can I contribute to make this happen?"

I have also seen some organizations print profesional photographs of their employees at work. The images are typically black and white super-sized photos of top employees doing their best work. Quite often these photos are captioned with the organization's motto or some inspiring word or phrase. Athletic organizations from the pros to high schools are using these inspirational photos to inspire team members and excite audiences.

Some athletes and sports teams I have worked with have vision boards in their locker rooms. On it you will find newspaper clippings, a picture of the trophy or title they seek, pictures of celebrations, perfect athletic form, and more! I have seen athletes lose themselves for a moment staring into these boards. You can see the visualization taking place, and you can see them making an internal resolution right before you. What will you hang on your vision board?

Visualization is a key to leadership. A leader finds ways to help everyone see the future result of today's hard work.

Dream Books: You need some place to write down your dreams personally as well. Some people call them journals, some call them vision books, I have a friend that calls his a dream book. Just like with the vision board, you can write things down you want and even paste pictures. It can even be a journal app on your smart phone. You just need a place to work on that vision.

You Need an Action Statement: Most organizations only focus on the vision statement, but you also need an action statement. The vision statement is what you are striving for overall, but the action statement is what you are committed to doing each day to make the vision a reality.

Become Positively Discontented: You have to possess positive discontent. What does that mean? It simply means you can never become completely satisfied with what you have accomplished. You cannot be satisfied, because satisfaction leads to stopping your growth. You can celebrate. You can be happy. You can mark it off your dream list, but by all means keep moving forward. Be discontented in a positive way. I have read books about college and professional coaches who are flying home from winning the championship and they pull out their journals and begin planning for the next season. Wow! What a commitment!

I have also seen leaders, athletes, and professionals hit an actual point of depression after completing a goal because they don't know where to go next. Also begin setting the next goal just before finishing a current goal. Keep moving!

Pleasant dissatisfaction is just you saying, "Things aren't where I want them to be yet." Satisfaction is a killer. Sure you need to celebrate your victories, but a leader is seldom content. There is always room for growth and improvement. Celebrate and then organize a new vision.

"Managers help people see themselves as they are. Leaders help people see themselves better than they are."
~ **Jim Rohn**

Build More Leaders!

Do you really want your organization to be successful? Are you prepared to help build other leaders? Where do leaders stand in the responsibility of creating other leaders? Weigh these questions carefully. Consider the similarities and differences between being a leader and creating other leaders.

I wonder how you answered these questions. Each says much about you and your future as a leader, as well as the success of your organization.

I hope you choose to build other leaders. An organization's success and the building of other leaders go hand in hand. If you are leading correctly and well, you are not only setting an excellent role model for future leaders, you are actually helping others become leaders.

For me the answer is simple; I want to raise leaders. I want those I work alongside to be prepared for anything, to make a difference, and live a life of purpose.

If you really want to help nurture a leader, you need to make three clear commitments:

1. **I will educate others about leadership.** Leadership really needs to be taught. It amazes me how many people don't understand this simple truth. If you want your teammate or colleague to become a leader, surround her with leadership resources. These can be books, audio, video, and so much more. This includes the comments you make about leaders in front of her. This includes the leadership examples *you* take on as well. If you don't serve a leadership role, those you hope to nurture into leaders probably won't either.

2. **I will provide others with leadership mentors.** A mentor is the greatest gift you can provide. Mentors can arrive in many fashions. Set it up. Mentoring must be one-on-one, consistent, and have a clear purpose.

3. **I will encourage others to lead.** If you want leaders you must allow them to accept leadership roles and encourage them. You can't do everything yourself. They will not get it right the first time either. They will need to make several attempts at it. It may require some extra responsibilities on your part, and may create a little unwanted drama, but leaders are made during the moments of discontent, not harmony. It will be worth it.

With the proper support, education, and mentoring they will fail their way to becoming a successful leader. Sadly, some finally receive an opportunity to lead, but have not received any education or mentoring about leadership, and fail so badly they vow to never lead again. I understand I need to listen to the types of leadership roles others are interested in, and at other times I will need to encourage possible leadership roles for them.

Clarity: Be clear in the purpose you set in the vision. Ask, "What do we want to do better than anyone else?" Having a vision is about knowing what you want. We need to revisit that vision often because the needs and busyness of the day can cloud the vision and take us off track. If you can't understand the vision you have written or shared, then neither can anyone else. Simplify it. Make it clear.

Size: Your vision does not have to be HUGE. Your organization needs to improve. You need to improve. You don't have to change the world, just serve it well. Keep your vision expanding and aim to make a difference.

"Every age needs men who will redeem the time by living with a vision of things that are to be."
~Adlai Stevenson

The Size of a Vision:

I recently journaled a list of the most influential people from my past and present. I attempted to record how their lives have impacted mine and what I learned from each. While there were a few common denominators, one really stood out amongst them all; each taught me that *the little things in life matter.*

It seems each influential person in my life attempted, in his or her own way, to encourage me to take care of the small matters because they add up and make big changes in our lives. My parents, teachers, coaches, and mentors all stressed this principle and I couldn't be more thankful. I have found that much of my success in life is due to this very simple truth.

As a coach, teacher, father, and speaker, I have passed along this valued lesson. On the football field we stressed the importance of each and every step and motion of the body to running a play successfully. The athletes had to actually complete a stop-motion series of steps, and they had to call them out as they progressed. In the classroom, the successful student is the one who takes care of the small matters in an assignment or project. At home I have taught my daughters to take care of problems before they get a chance to grow. Even in my relationships, the greatest affection and interest has always come from the small matters of thank-you notes, phone calls, and simple pleasantries.

Truly, taking care of the small things in life has much to do with compassion and discipline. *Be compassionate enough to allow the small things to matter* and *be disciplined enough to see them through*. The good habits of exercise, saving money, prayer, reading, and eating healthy become habits with the very smallest of beginnings.

Years ago I read a great book by legendary basketball coach John Wooden. In the book, Coach Wooden explains how his first lesson for his top NCAA basketball recruits (each of whom was recruited by countless schools, and each having played basketball incredibly well since they could run) was to teach them the proper way to tie their shoes. Yes, tie their shoes! Coach Wooden knew a shoe could and would come untied during a big game, at a crucial time, and that single factor could decide the outcome. It's the little things that truly matter most.

One of my favorite movies, *The Shawshank Redemption*, focuses heavily on this theme. Actor Tim Robbins plays the part of Andy, a wrongly imprisoned man who impacts the lives of everyone at The Shawshank Prison through his small, yet consistent actions. Andy makes some amazing accomplishments, and an incredible escape from a corrupt prison and a wrongful sentence, simply by focusing and mastering the very smallest of details. Watch this movie. A little effort compounded daily can go a long way to bringing your vision to reality.

Let us be reminded that the smallest of snow flakes that land on the mountain top combine with others building layer upon layer, melting and moving downward to become some of the most powerful rivers on the planet. These rivers carve their way through stone, and over time they leave their lasting impression on our planet. Small things really do add up. Little things really do matter.

Let's give these small matters the attention they deserve and wait and see if they do not in fact lead to an amazing change in ourselves.

"In this life we cannot do great things. We can only do small things with great love."
~ Mother Teresa

Visions are Powered by Questions: What are some of the little things in our lives that need greater attention? What small thing can you begin today that will make a difference over time? How can you articulate your mission regularly, passionately? What questions should you be asking to drive your vision?

"I skate to where the puck is going, not to where the puck has been."
~ Wayne Gretzky

Vision allows the leader to be innovative and create the results that matter. If you can't see what you want to accomplish, how will you know if you ever make it? You need a plan. You need a vision.

Creating a Powerful Vision: Your vision as a leader cannot be reduced to a corporate mission statement. Your vision is about becoming a better you, not the best on the planet. Your vision is about what you have to offer. Your organization's vision is a passionate statement of how it is unique and how it is making a difference in the world.

You know you have the right vision when it keeps you moving forward. You know you have the right vision when you share it and others want to learn more and become involved. Visions are both the anchor that keeps you and the organization aligned, while allowing itself to be trimmed and fitted from time to time to remain engaging and timely.

•••

If you want to create a powerful vision, you must ask powerful questions. Ask yourself:

What do I do best?
What am I about?
What do I stand for?
What will I always defend?
What matters most in my life?
What word or words would I want others to use to describe me?
What legacy do I want to leave behind?
What do I enjoy doing?
What are my strengths?
What traits do I admire most in others?
What traits disgust me?

I could generate a list like this for a very long time, but I will stop here. You get the idea. What I am attempting to uncover in this exercise are core beliefs. A creed, if you will. Some people call it a mission statement. I've never liked exercises in creating mission statements much because we always crafted something that didn't sound like us. When I wrote down my beliefs and core statement, they sound like me, because it *is* me. It's the vision of the man I want to become. My creed or core statement for my business is what I want it to become. I have creeds in many different areas of life. I have crafted a short core statement for my physical self, spiritual self, fatherhood, and many other areas. I reflect on these often. They guide and center me to what I want to become.

I recommend that you create your own creed or core statement. Make it sound like you. Spend time on it. Keep it short. Reflect and alter it as you see fit. Once you have it, stick to it. Spend time with it daily in relfection.

Most of my core values and creed come from the people, organizations, and situations that influenced my life. Even horrible examples of leadership influenced me. I learned what I didn't want to become!

Start defining your core beliefs, creed, and vision today. They will guide you for the rest of your life making every decision and obstacle easier.

A good process for a leader to bring a vision to reality is the following:

- Start with a dream. Dream big!
- Next, begin drafting your vision. Your vision is more reasonable than your dream, but still inspiring.
- The vision should be transformed into a mission statement. A mission statement is something everyone can understand and contribute to.
- The mission statement is broken into goals. Goals are doable tasks that have deadlines.
- Your goals become your prioritized to-do list. Your to-do list consists of actions you can accomplish each day to move closer to the due date of your goal.

This is how you accomplish your vision.

A strong vision is paramount to leadership, and now you have a better understanding of how to create and use vision as a leader.

Commitment 5

The Fifth Leadership Commitment
I will lead with an inspiring vision.

Knowing that vision is the guidance system of all leadership, I will create, embrace, and share an exciting and meaningful vision, with my team, often and with passion. I will help others see their role and contribution to the overall vision.

Four-minute speed art tribute to one of our great innovators.

CHAPTER 9

Authenticity

Living an authentic life is paramount to maintaining your credibility as a leader and leaving a lasting impact on others. Authenticity is the glue that holds leadership together; without it a leader falls apart.

If you assembled all of the people you know, together in one room, would they describe the same person? Authenticity isn't about being perfect, but it has everything to do with trust, integrity, and loyalty. Living an authentic life is paramount to maintaing your credibility as a leader and leaving a lasting impact on others. We trust and admire those who live authentic lives. Leaders are people who live by a set of core values regardless of the circumstances, and regardless who is around.

Do you act the same way regardless of who is around? Or are you a different person to different people? As a teacher and coach I have observed that student athletes often act differently depending on who is watching them. Even within some families we see behavior changes, and issues of integrity based on who is around at the time. I have had many discussions with teachers and coaches that describe very different observations of the same student, athlete, or colleague.

Authenticity is about who you say you are, who people say you are, and who you really are. Tell me what you truly value and I'll tell you what kind of person you will become.

Authenticity is the glue that holds leadership together. Without it a leader falls apart. Nothing will weaken your impact more, or destroy your accomplishments faster than a breach of trust or a lapse in your integrity.

Authenticity acts as the life support system for the five previously discussed elements of leadership. If you have a great attitude on the job, yet return home and whine and complain, your leadership suffers and becomes vulnerable. The same is true for wisdom, tenacity, vision, and communication. Work hard to keep each strong, regardless of the time of day, situation, or environment you work. Authenticity is all about consistency of character. Perfection cannot be achieved, but progress is to be expected.

BE AUTHENTIC!

In the last chapter I discussed the importance of creating a strong vision. I guided you through some questions to help you determine your core beliefs and form your own personal creed or set of beliefs. A leader needs to act consistently and within his or her established beliefs and creed. When we act contrary to our core we lose credibility with those we lead. We lose our influence.

You may find yourself a little uncomfortable reading this chapter because you behave a little differently within different groups of people. There's nothing wrong with that. I do the same. We know who we can joke around with and with whom we need to be more serious. What cannot change are our values. We must carry with us a set of core values that are unwavering. A little change in your willingness to joke around is okay, but a change in what is the right thing to do or the wrong thing to do is unacceptable and a contradiction to authenticity

Everything you do and say matters. If you are going to be successful as a leader you better have a solid understanding of who you are, the values for which you and your organization stand, and the principles that guide you and your organization. You also better have a solid understanding of what you and your organization will refuse to associate with and partake. Make these values part of your personal vision and creed. Understand them completely. Keep them in front of you and those you lead daily. I mean this. It is important that your personal values align with those of your organization. The same is true for all members part of that organization. If there is a mismatch then it needs to be corrected within the individual, not by bending your values. If you aren't doing this, or believe you cannot do this then you better be working on it or you will fail as a leader and face some very tough patches in your life.

If you have a strong sense of values and authenticity, and by this I mean you know who you are and what you stand for, as well as the vision and principles that guide your organization, tough decisions won't be as tough.

These really do need to be written out. Yes, they can be a part of your vision statement from the last chapter, but I think it is very important that you make a list, a creed, if you will, of what you stand for as a person, and as a leader. By writing it down you can see the person you want to become, and it makes it easier to stand for what you say you really do.

As a young Scout and student I was asked to memorize certain creeds and oaths. There is an absolute brilliance to reciting the Scout Oath and the Scout Creed out loud regularly, and the same is true for your vision and values today. In Scouting, we had a motto, we had a slogan, we had an oath, and we had twelve guiding points by which to live. We were required to memorize these points, oaths, creeds, and mottos. We were required to teach them. We were required to live them. It was the standard by which we were measured as a Scout. I can still recite all to this day. I live by all to this day. It works. Write your's down. Fine tune it. Memorize it. Teach it. Live it.

Leadership is not about the authority we have over other people;

leadership is about influence. Our ability to influence others is the key measurement of our effectiveness as a leader. When a leader's authenticity is damaged it immediately and directly impacts his ability to influence. Great care and effort needs to be applied in maintaining our authenticity as a leader. If we don't know what we stand for, how will others? If we cannot follow the standards we set and are supposed to represent, how can we lead others to follow them?

An employee, a teammate, your child, and anyone you lead will cast aside any influence you had when your authenticity has been damaged, especially if you don't take immediate steps to correct and rebuild it. When you fail to follow through on your principles or creed, acknowledge it, and let those you lead know how you are going to fix it so you are back on track. Leadership is not about being perfect or becoming perfect, but it is about improvement. When you make a mistake take the steps necessary to correct it. Authenticity is all about responsibility.

I have borrowed greatly from others in creating my set of core beliefs that guide my life. I lean heavily on the lessons I learned in the Boy Scouts, my Christian faith, the work ethic of the sports in which I have been involved, and the many leaders I have met throughout my life. I use their words to help craft my own. I encourage you to do the same. Distill the essence of your core values and the description of the leader you wish to become from all of the sources you admire. Share it with your inner circle, mentors, and those you admire. Adjust it accordingly.

One reason so many leaders fail at authenticity is that they do not surround themselves with authentic people. You've heard the cliche, "Lay down with dogs; wake up with fleas." It's true. You will take on the values and character of the people you spend the most time with each day. Surround yourself with authentic people.

"You are the average of the five people you spend the most time with."
~Jim Rohn

Loyalty vs. Authenticity

I have asked friends what qualities they believe to be most important in another individual. Time and time again I have heard loyalty to be the most sought after quality. When asked which is the greater quality I will wager most people will say loyalty over authenticity. I believe most do not understand what authenticity truly means. After much reflection and consideration, I completely understand the attraction to loyalty, but I am committed to placing authenticity above it. As an Eagle Scout, I know well that loyalty is one of the twelve points of the Scout Law. I admire loyalty and I do seek it from others, but it is not a virtue. Too often I have seen the trouble of blind loyalty. Those who pledge their allegiance to a person, rather than a quality, and they look the other way when someone does something unethical, out of their 'loyalty" to them.

A person with integrity knows right from wrong. When they live an authentic life they remain true to their integrity, not a person. People err. People fail. People harm. We are loyal to virtuous ideas, not people we like. Authenticity and integrity balance to what and to whom we are loyal. Authenticity in leadership keeps our loyalty on course.

When I talk with teenagers I am often surprised when they tell me they would not tell the parent of a friend if they knew that friend had been drinking or using drugs, or doing other dangerous acts. They argue that it is wrong to 'snitch' or turn in a friend. This troubles me. A true friend, and a true leader seeks the best in others. A leader wants to help bring out the best in others and help them. Informing an adult about a possible life-threatening situation is not only the right thing to do, it is our responsibility. It's not only the right thing to do, it is an example of leadership at its best.

Sure we want leaders to be loyal. Loyalty is a great quality, but not loyalty to people. Our loyalty should be to ideals, virtues, and codes of conduct. If someone is violating an oath of office, amteam code of conduct, or showing bad moral judgment, even if and especially if that person is a higher ranking official, as leaders we must help them right their course and realign themselves to their vision and code of ethics.

How do we seek and obtain authenticity?

Write down your core values! Write down a set of core values that you wish to obtain, or adopt some from others.

•••

Accountability and Mentoring: Have an accountability partner or mentor. I talked a great deal about mentoring in the earlier chapter on wisdom. An accountability partner is very similar to a mentor. In this day and age our mentor and accountability partners can sometimes even have meetings via video conference check-ins and other means, but in person meetings are still most beneficial. These meetings are times where you can sit down and bounce ideas off of someone, discuss troubling situations, talk about areas you feel you were unable to give your best. This person should check in with you periodically and ask you vital questions based on your core standards. When choosing a mentor make sure you choose someone with great integrity. Choose someone you trust. Choose someone you admire.

It has become clear to me that those who are the least authentic in life and lack integrity are the ones who are quick to attack and aim to ruin the reputation of others. They would rather put others down than do the work to build up their reputation. They are superficial and believe getting a hair cut or a new coat will change everyone's impression of them. These people don't understand and respect authenticity.

It isn't something that is a part of their life, so they can easily sling mud at others in hopes that it sticks. These same people believe that leadership is simply a title or a position bestowed upon them, rather than something that is earned each and every day through service. I cannot stand inauthentic leaders.

"A great way to remember who you are is to remember who you admire."
~Steve Jobs

Who are your heroes? Who do you look up to? What qualities do you wish you possessed? What qualities do you admire in others? What do you admire most about the great men and women of history? These are but a few guiding questions to help you draft your creed that will govern your leadership style.

While stressing authenticity it is important for me to emphasize that we want to be authentic to our best qualities. We seek improvement. Some may think it unauthentic to try to become a better person. "Hey! That's not you," they think. "You are trying to become something you're not. You're not being authentic." Please know those other people are wrong. We are made to be more and become more than we currently are at any moment. If we are taking breaths of air, then our work in this world is unfinished. Authenticity is about being true to your best self, not your carefree whims. Authenticity is about discipline. Authenticity is about being true to the values you aspire within you, and making choices that lead you more closely to their attainment.

When we make a poor choice we take two steps back from our authentic self, the person we are destined to become. When we make a good choice we take one step forward to the life we were meant to live, and the leader we are meant to become.

Authenticity isn't about becoming someone else you admire. It's about admiring the person you are becoming. Many people will tell you they are satisfied about being the person they already are, eating chips and watching television for six hours a day, but they're not. They use food and television as a diversion from the life they are currently living. Inside they know they were meant for more.

Get Back On Track: Be quick to correct a lapse in authenticity, especially your own. Do not assume others didn't notice. You aren't correcting it for them anyway, you are correcting it for yourself, for your fellow team members, for the vision, for those who served before you, for those who will come after you, for the family members that would be impacted. Being a leader carries a great weight of responsibility and great efforts must be made to uphold your character and integrity. Authentic leadership is the admiration of all.

A friend of mine graduated from the Naval Academy, where authenticity is ingrained into each and every graduate. We went to a fast food restaurant with some friends once, and he was given the incorrect change. He was calculating the error as we were leaving the restaurant. He told us he had to go back in and fix the error. A buddy of ours pointed out that the error was in his favor. He was given too much money back! He replied, "I know! I have to get back in there." The overpayment was for less than a dollar, but he explained that someone at some point was going to have to account for that money, and that doing the right thing, **every time**, is what's important. My friend believed if he overlooked the error in his favor, despite how small it might seem, it might start a habit of allowing him to overlook more. Would he start justifying more, and allowing what was right and wrong to blur? I think my friend made the right call. Even the smallest lapses in moral judgment plant the seeds for our authenticity to be challenged another day. Constant corrections and adjustments keep us on course.

A man with integrity doesn't do right once in awhile, not most of the time, and not just when others see it. The authentic leader does the right thing every single time. Sure, he will make mistakes, but once he knows he has, he will immediately move to correct it.

During my college football practices our team had to run warm-up laps around the field. While running those laps a few of the guys would round off the corners of the field. They didn't go all the way around the corner, and shaved off a few feet and some time and energy. They didn't stay outside the white line like we were told. It was easier to round off the corner.

Well, our line coach would yell. "Hey! You cheat on these laps and you'll cheat on your wife! You cheat on these laps and you'll cheat your whole life." It had a nice rhyme and by midway through camp we'd all repeat it once he started and whoever rounded a corner would stop immediately.

I still remember that lesson today. There is a lot of truth to it. To cheat in life you have to start somewhere. I'm pretty certain that the guy with a machine gun robbing a bank probably started smaller, and this isn't his first time doing something dishonest. Did he take a nickel off his brother's dresser when they were little? Did he steal a paper-clip from a teacher's desk in school? Graduate to taking his classmates' lunch money? It had to start somewhere!

You aren't born with integrity. Sure we're innocent enough when we are little. Integrity, trustworthiness, loyalty, are qualities you build upon your entire life. They're like bank accounts. Every time you keep your word, and do the right thing you make a deposit. When you lie and cheat you make a withdrawal and, well, you could potentially go bankrupt. Work at being authentic.

We expect athletes to take responsibility for their actions during a competition. Nothing upsets me more or disappoints me more when an athlete blames someone else for a mistake. Nothing makes me more proud when a person immediately owns up to their mistakes. Let's face it, mistakes are going to happen. If you're not making mistakes you aren't doing enough. Take responsibility.

I admire companies more when they apologize and admit when there's a problem. I want them to quickly follow with a notice that they are going to get to the bottom of what went wrong. I want them to say that their customers deserve better. I like that straightforward leadership. I want that transparency and authenticity.

To lead for any duration a leader must possess authenticity. To be truly authentic we must practice it at every moment of every day. Nothing will weaken your impact more or destroy your accomplishments more quickly than a breach of trust and a lapse in your integrity.

Take Responsibility: One of the biggest disappointments I have experienced was finding out that a favorite mentor was not the man of character that I believed he was. Before I become too critical of this man to emphasize my point on authenticity, let me stress a couple of very important points. First, I have always been taught to judge a man by his achievements and not his failures, but most importantly not to judge. Second, this mentor was instrumental in my success as an athlete and had a huge influence on the formation of my character. Quite simply, I would not be that man I am today without his guidance. With this being noted, I watched this man's life collapse because of his inability to live a life of authenticity. He presented himself to society as a man of character, discipline, and honor, but behaved privately in a manner contrary to the virtues he taught. It eventually cost him his credibility, his marriage, and his job.

My mentor identified a talent within me that I did not even know that I had. He spent time with me and helped me to discipline myself. He took an interest when no one else did, and even more importantly he gave me an opportunity to compete and perform when no else thought I was ready. He held me to a higher standard. He praised me when I succeeded and encouraged me when I struggled. I thought the world of him. He was without a doubt a great leader, but his leadership was short-lived due to a fissure developing in his authenticity.

Sometime in my early adulthood, I heard of his demise and the troubles he faced. I attempted to return the support and return the encouragement he had given me years earlier. It is very difficult to support someone when they are accused of a wrong. To my surprise he told me point-blank to not be involved with him because he was in fact guilty of what he was accused of doing and he didn't want my reputation blemished. He leaned on the old adage, "He made his bed, and now he had to lay in it." I was in shock.

To my surprise, however, he provided me with another great life lesson. He took responsibility for his actions.

I was pleased when he eventually turned his life around. He is doing great. I know that he eventually was able to return to the work he loved and was reunited with his family due to accepting responsibility for his actions and working to make it right. What a lesson I received in authenticity!

Friends walk toward you when you need them: best friends run.

Living an authentic life is paramount to maintaining your credibility as a leader and leaving a lasting impact on others. You cannot lead by telling others, "Do as I say, not as I do." That will not work.

Tests of Authenticity: It's easy to be a good automobile driver when the weather is great and everyone else on the road is driving sensibly. The true test of a driver however may very well be when the roads are slick, there's an accident up ahead, and everyone just hit their brakes.

Likewise, your authenticity will be tested. Situations at your organization will at times turn for the worse and you will be faced with choices. Sometimes a choice contrary to your values presents itself as the easiest choice. It looks like an easy way out. That's never the right choice. Always choose what's right, even when it's hard. Choose right, especially when it's hard.

Speak up for others when they are wronged, even if it makes for an uncomfortable situation for yourself. Looking the other way and not getting involved is not being authentic to your morals and ethics, nor yourself. How could you carry on knowing someone had been wronged? I couldn't. Always speak up. That's leadership.

Transparency

I loved being a football coach. Some of my greatest memories are from coaching. I'm proud of that service, the boys I coached, the men I coached with, and the other coaches I met.

I got to meet a lot of college coaches over those years. We went to coaching clinics and conferences, and I have to admit I always wanted to meet the head coach of my favorite teams. One such coach I met was one of college football's best. Another was from a smaller school but has since climbed the ladder and become one of the top coaches in the game as well. I will keep the names of both coaches to myself.

Both of these coaches left their teams around the same time to coach somewhere else. The way they went about it though is a lesson in leadership and demonstrates the importance of authenticity.

The first coach sat his team down and told them he was interested in coaching at his dream school. He loved where he was, but he, like them, had dreams. He told them that if he was offered to take the job he would meet with them and let them know before anyone else knew, especially the media. They appreciated his candor and transparency. They even encouraged and supported him to pursue his dream. He did in fact take the job, and his former team supported him and backed his decision to coach at his dream school. They felt, and rightfully so, that they were included in his decision.

The other coach handled applying for a new job quite differently. He interviewed at several schools, without his team's knowledge, and took a job without even letting anyone know he was considering leaving. The news of the hire hit the media and got back to his current team before he had a chance to talk with them. His team was in shock and disbelief. I remember watching the news one night seeing the captain of his team tell the cameraman, "I won't believe it until I hear coach tell us himself."

I understand both coaches' desire to advance their careers, but clearly the former handled the situation better than the latter.

Remain true to the values you request and demand of others. As leaders we need to pursue our dreams and visions, and we need to support the dreams of those we lead, even if it means someone leaving for another organization. It's *how* you make these decisions that underscore your authenticity and integrity. Strive to be transparent, honorable, and the leader of your organization at all times.

Praise and Responsibility: I always admired Harry Truman's "The Buck Stops Here!" mantra. The leaders of our current culture are too quick to divert the blame to someone else and too quick to pin the praise on their chests.

Carry responsibility for your actions and the actions of those you lead.

I was blessed to have been a small part in a very successful coaching program. I was surrounded by giants of leadership and scholars of the game. If I made any contribution to our success it was minuscule in comparison to what those fellow coaches sacrificed and gave. I will always treasure those memories of coaching.

I recently looked back at my football career and realized that I have been involved in the sport in some shape or form for over thirty years. In the game, it's all about the football. Everyone is trying to get the darn ball, and the shape of that ball is just awkward. It just doesn't bounce the same way twice or roll in a straight line. There is a lot of responsibility in the handling of that ball from the time it is snapped from the center to the quarterback, handed off to one of the backs, or thrown to a receiver.

Every athlete on the field must be a leader and take responsibility for that football. No one is given permission to disown their responsibility to a turnover or mistake. Eleven men are on the field and all share in the responsibility of what happens out there. If that ball bounces a funny way or a play goes sour, everyone needs to be aware and take action.

Lets face it, mistakes are going to happen. If you're not making mistakes you aren't doing enough. Take responsibility. If that ball is stripped loose jump on it, don't stand there pointing the finger.

> *"Leadership is doing what is right when no one is watching."*
> **—George Van Valkenburg**

Dissatisfaction rarely seems positive, but you should be pleased with the progress you are making, but never become complacent and stagnant. Always strive to improve yourself as a leader. You are constantly becoming something else. That something is either for the better or for worse. Never be satisfied with where you are in life. Strive to become the best you can be. If you value honesty, and you believe you are honest, don't rest on your laurels, work at being even more honest. The same is true of all the values and principles you admire and wish to be attributed to your leadership.

As I mentioned earlier, I am proud of my experience in Scouting. I earned the rank of Eagle and I still hold that accomplishment in the highest of regards. For starters, there are very few people that will stick with something that long and work that hard. Scouting taught me to be steadfast and diligent.

It would take an entire series of books to sum up the vast knowledge I learned in Scouting, but there are a couple of stories I must share with you.

When you are in Scouts you are given the option to subscribe to the magazine *Boy's Life*. *Boy's Life* is unique because it is written for the audience of Scouts. The stories, jokes, cartoons, advertisements, and articles are all written for young men interested in becoming their personal best.

There was one particular section in the magazine that I always turned to first. It was a cartoon. I'm sure that's no surprise to those of you that have seen one of my performances. This cartoon, however, was unique. It wasn't funny. It was serious. Each month the artist would illustrate a true heroic story featuring a real Boy Scout. Every strip ended the same way, with an illustration of that young man in uniform having a heroic medal pinned on his chest. I wanted to be that scout. I thought about it all the time. I dreamt about it. I daydreamed about it.

The sad truth is that I was always sorta hoping something bad would happen so I could jump up and be the hero. (I know. I know. That' s just not right, but I was just a boy at the time.) I would look out at frozen ponds searching for someone to save. I looked for accidents everywhere I went. How immature of me! I did become an Eagle Scout, but I never did get an award for bravery and heroism. Thank goodness!

Most boys dream about being heroes, and I suppose that is admirable to a point. I never had my cartoon in *Boy's Life* magazine. I realized of course, as I matured, that it's not about the recognition, nor the award. It is about action, bravery, and humility. I was trained to respond. I learned to be humble. I was honored to have learned what to do and know how to react when needed. The focus is to be a servant leader. Those we serve are the highlight, we are the background.

Too often I think people do the right thing for the wrong reason. We shouldn't do right to receive recognition. Don't do what is right for just personal advancement. Don't do what is right for just the recognition. That is not authenticity. Being authentic is doing what's right because that is who you are, why you're here, and what you do. You do it because it's second nature to you.

Scouting was also a great teacher of goal setting. I learned the importance of setting and obtaining goals. I learned how to break a problem down into doable steps. I felt the importance of recognition and learned to recognize others. I was taught the importance of running a meeting and being prepared. Pick up a *Boy Scout Handbook* from any decade and you will see the magic of servant leadership on every page.

What Others Think of You: There were times when I was younger that I worried too much about what others thought, and I didn't attempt opportunities that I really wanted to try. Sometimes I still weigh too heavily the opinion of others, but only because I always want to do a good job. Authenticity also means following your own path and marching to the beat of your own drum. When we allow the opinions of others to hold us back from our dreams and goals we are stepping away from an authentic life and authentic leadership. Every time we follow through on something we really want to achieve and try, we are taking a step toward an authentic life.

Starting my own business was a risk. It has taught me much. We need to take risks. We need to be heard.

Leaders make decisions.

Each and every time a leader makes a decision they are impacting a life.

Apply the 'Domino' or 'Butterfly' effect and the number of lives impacted by a leader's single decision is sometimes mesmerizing.

That is why leaders need to: respond rather than react, seek wisdom, listen to counsel, and reflect frequently.

Once a decision is made, however, it is not final. Leaders must be decisive and firm, but when a poor decision is made, and it happens, it is a leader's duty to make it right.

I firmly believe that leaders must take the motto "We'll make it right!" to heart; it's never too late to right a wrong.

I learned the correct way to make an apology from Dr. Randy Pausch. In his book, *The Last Lecture*, Pausch states that a great apology is made up of three important qualities: 1) Saying you are sorry. 2) Promising that it won't happen again. 3) Asking what you can do to make it better.

Apologies can at times cause more harm than good if attempted poorly. Step three of the apology, is of the utmost importance. Step three is all about making things right.

As a leader you have the ability to right a wrong, and you have the responsibility. Too often leaders allow a poor decision to go uncorrected. Poor leaders are worried how it will look to others if they admit they were wrong. Cowards.

When I am about to do business with someone, and they tell me that they will make it right if things don't work out the way they promised, that reassures me. It's even better if they have a proven track record showing that they make things right. No product, no company, no service, and no leader, is going to be right 100% of the time. It's impossible. So, what are you going to do as a leader when a mistake is made? Well, the answer to that will speak volumes of your leadership style, and volumes about you as a person.

Apple is admired by me and millions of others, but even their competitors recognize that they make things right when there is a problem. Apple has won repeated awards for customer service. They correct the wrong, replace the defect, ship the replacement, or extend the agreement.

I'm amazed at how many companies don't do this. They simply continue on and ignore the mistake. I have even had customer service calls where a company will admit that there really is a mistake, but refuse to correct it. Wow! What exactly does that say about you as a person, your corporation, or your leadership? Make it right!

Some leaders will argue that it is too costly to make it right; I'd argue the opposite. Nothing is more expensive than letting a wrong continue. I mean that both metaphorically and financially. You will lose your authenticity as a leader, lose respect, lose support, lose money, and just plain lose.

We'll Make it Right! Don't just say it, do it.

Some time ago, Netflix, the world's largest online movie rental service changed it's user agreement. It failed miserably. They finally admitted they made a mistake, but… they did nothing to make it right. They could have flipped a switch and offered a free video, and given something, but they chose to do nothing and it didn't work for them at all. They lost subscribers and their stock plummeted. When did things change for Netflix? When they made it right. Their CEO admitted the wrong and made corrections. Up went their authenticity and everything else followed.

Making a bad decision is forgivable and easy to recover from when you make a move to correct it; in fact correcting it adds to your authenticity. No one should expect perfection from a leader. We want leaders who fix the wrongs and aim for progress. We do not want someone that ignores a wrong, or covers it up.

A friend of mine told me a story about how a board member 'let go' an employee. The board member said he had always regretted that decision. My friend, a leader, said… (you guessed it) "make it right." They did and all involved were happy for it; its never too late. Never.

Let people know that you are going to work hard to earn back their confidence and make certain this problem doesn't happen again. Make your critics part of your team, because making things right makes them the beta testers. When you follow through, they will sing your praises even louder. Don't however, just give people lip-service. You must work hard to maintain your integrity and authenticity. You are never, ever too big or important to call a client or customer yourself. Don't pass this responsibility on to others. In fact, making the call in person to correct a problem is the way to go.

In some situations you cannot win a customer or an employee back, but you should try. If you have made a sincere attempt to make things right, and they aren't accepting your sincere and fair request, then it is time to move on. Leaders must know and repeat to themselves every day, "I can't control what others think or believe, but I can work hard to make myself and situations better." Do your best and move forward. Don't burn bridges; just do the next best action.

I have seen too many leaders actually believe they should not go back and correct a wrong. I write this for the them, and our future leaders.

Always make it right.

In some situations a public apology is needed. Years ago a young coach shared a story with me about how a parent humiliated him in front of a team of boys he was coaching. The parent criticized and ridiculed the young coach in a truly awful manner. Hours later the man approached the young coach in a parking lot alone and offered an **insincere** apology. When the man was asked by the coach whether he could come to a practice and offer the same apology in front of the boys who witnessed his verbal assault, the man refused. The apology should have been made in front of all of those that witnessed the verbal attack, not in a vacant parking lot.

We must strive for authenticity in our lives.

A man should be remembered for his best actions, not his worst.

No one asks us to forget, but only to forgive. The greatest gift you can ever offer anyone in this life is a second chance.

Would Steve Jobs Consider You a Bozo?

The world is filled with admirers of Steve Jobs, and rightfully so. The man was an incredible visionary, innovator, speaker, businessman, leader, and communicator. His impact has left little untouched. One overlooked talent though, was his use of simple language to convey his passion for a product or service. How many times did we hear him say, "insanely great, phenomenal, awesome, revolutionary, amazing, and of course magical?"

His word choice was in sync with his passion for minimalism in design and the simple elegance of his presentation. Uncomplicated. Straightforward. Direct. Powerful. The advertisements, stores, packaging, and even his dress embodied this motif.

He chose simple words, but words powerful in their connotations. They were chosen with care. They were delivered with passion. They told a story.

My favorite term that Jobs used was when he called someone or their idea a Bozo.

Bozo was a term Steve would use to describe someone that just didn't get it. A bozo to him was someone that was more interested in the bureaucracy of business rather than innovation. A bozo was someone that was ineffective and someone that wasn't authentic. A bozo was someone who focused on what wasn't important. Basically a bozo was anyone Steve didn't respect.

I recently read an article about his use of the term bozo at his second company NeXt. According to NeXt employees, you could go from bozo to genius in months if you eventually *got it* and performed. (Better yet, outperformed.) And I am sure you could probably drop back down again too.

Many think Steve burned bridges, but I don't think that is the case at all. Sure, he was competitive and occasionally became upset, but I still remember the shock I had, and later conceded to the brilliance of his move, when he partnered Apple with Microsoft. When you consider all of the deals he made with the record industry, artists, television companies, and publishers, you realize he built far more bridges than he ever burned.

Steve Jobs had standards, incredibly high ones, for himself, his staff, and the corporations he created. The results speak for themselves. Bozos either don't have standards or they break them. Bozos lack vision or don't follow it. Bozos place business over delivering a quality service or product. The bottom line: bozos are people who aren't authentic.

Don't want to be a bozo? Do the following:

- Be original. Don't steal the work of others. Create. Don't copy. March to the beat of your own drum.
- Set high standards and hold others to high standards.
- Be more proud of what you didn't do, than what you did.
- Have a vision. Focus on it and chase it down.
- Understand and emphasize the relationship between product/ service and the client.
- Know the story behind why you do what you do.
- Do what you love.
- Give more than you take.
- Ship quality.

These are just my observations of a man I never met, but a man who impacted my life more than most of those whom I have.

I will work hard not to be a bozo. I will work hard for anyone except a bozo.

Customer Service: If you have a slogan...

A while back I went through an uncomfortable customer service experience with an automotive company and the handling of their recall of my vehicle. While I understand recalls happen and improve safety, I believe corporations should recognize some very basic principles in the handling of their customer service. Customer service is paramount.

Here is my advice about how you can improve your customer service and lead with authenticity:

1. **Care:** Customer service is truly that simple. Show the customer that you genuinely care about them, and that you're not just trying to cover your butt. Recognize the importance of the customer's time, and acknowledge its value. Show the customer you care about them, not the problem, not the product, not who's right, but the individual customer. Care.

2. **Answer the Customer's Question:** Don't answer questions so guardedly and evasively that the consumer is confused. Don't make the customer go through a series of handlers before getting someone that can actually answer the question. Respond to the customer's questions timely. Unanswered questions makes the customer feel unimportant. Ultimately the customer just wants to know if someone is doing something.

3. **Ask The Customer The Magic Question:** What can I do to make this better? You don't necessarily have to give what they ask, but if it is the right thing to do, I hope you consider it. The customer will at least feel as if they were heard. Perhaps the customer doesn't even know what they want, and this line of ques-

tioning will lead to a solution. Listen to the customer. Keeping records does not make good customer service. Just because you took notes about our conversation does not prove to me anything is being done, nor that you even listened.

4. **Offer Something The Customer Cannot Obtain or Achieve on Her Own:** Personalize the experience. Offer to do something the customer cannot do on their own. The automotive company offered to call the local dealer for me and the car rental place and make an inquiry, but I had already done that. Living in a small town I asked them not to bother the dealer because the recall wasn't his fault. I even asked them to document that request. It was overlooked and it made me uncomfortable with the dealer. the customer. Don't offer to do something I can do on my own, provide me with something beyond my ability.

5. **If your Company has a Slogan or Motto, Live up to it:** On this automotive website it said: "Brand Name: Drive one." Yet during the three months I was without my vehicle I was never offered one, even after I requested one. The automative company hired a car rental company to provide me with a rental vehicle. Their slogan is "Brand Name: We'll Pick You Up." Yet, when I called them to schedule a pick up, they told me I was out of their delivery range. What!? If you have a slogan, live up to it. Both companies failed.

I wish this automotive company well, in fact I own stock in the company, and I applaud the workers that build their amazing vehicles. However, this automotive company's future success, and that of any company is not solely in their product, but also in their customer service. Sadly, my next vehicle will not be from them, simply because they had me test drive a competitor's vehicle for the three months of recall repair, and I fell in love with the rental made by their competitor. Recalls and repairs happen, but take care of the customer. For better or for worse, the experience will be memorable.

Leaders never blind side others.

This may be the most important lesson on authenticity.

A blind side is a cowardly attack that demonstrates an incapacity to communicate and an inability to make leadership decisions. It is an act committed out of fear, jealously, and anger. A blind side is a poor attempt to hide the inability to lead.

Those who choose the blind side willingly forgo the path of a leader. They would rather sneak behind-the-scenes, than sit down and have a discussion. They would rather plot, than plan. The higher the level of office, rank, title, or position, the more detrimental the act.

The world recognizes a blind side for what it is, wrong. Our history has been littered with them: the attack on Pearl Harbor in 1941 and the devastating destruction of The World Trade Towers in 2001 are known to all. Within the corporate world, the notorious ousting of Steve Jobs at Apple in 1985 has redefined leadership decisions and highlighted a return to ethical standards within the board room. The facade of leadership behind these infamous blind sides are viewed with contempt and outrage by the world and history, and in time each wrong was made right or avenged. Every. Single. Time.

A true leader can craft a thousand proposals to handle a situation, but a blind side is never one of them. A leader addresses challenges with communication, and a well-planned response. A leader creates options. A leader presides with dignity and honor. A leader offers counsel, an assessment, or intervention. A leader demonstrates innovation. A blind side is none of these.

Leaders are defined by their actions. What does a blind side convey? Not the qualities of leadership. A blind side affirms a weakness in character, a desire to harm, belittle, and embarrass. A blind side is wrong.

Only low-brow reality television offers a nod to the immaturity of a well-played blind side. There is no place for it among leaders. It is indefensible.

I have identified six essential elements of leadership in this book: attitude, wisdom, communication, tenacity, vision, and authenticity. A blind side negates them all. Yes, each and every one. I cannot be clearer: forbid it from your management and leadership staff. Admonish and shun those who use it. Anyone and everyone with any common sense will no longer trust a leader who blind sides. No defense, scenario, or lie can be crafted well enough to convince others of its necessity. Others will forever question, "How long will it **be** before he blind sides **me**?" Trust quickly fades, everyone questions the act, everyone watches their back, and a dark shadow of shame is cast on the organization.

Just because you can do something, doesn't mean you should. A leader never blindsides.

"Your time is limited, so don't waste it living someone else's life. Don't be trapped by dogma - which is living with the results of other people's thinking. Don't let the noise of others' opinions drown out your own inner voice. And most important, have the courage to follow your heart and intuition."
~Steve Jobs

Strive for authenticity in your life. Develop a written creed. Write down your standards. Identify and meet regularly with your accountability partner. Study the leaders you most admire. Work to become a great leader and person of integrity. Lead by your motto.

Leaders live by their word. Leaders must show they can be trusted, that they are honest, and dependable. Leaders cannot afford to make excuses or say they simply forgot. Leaders are allowed to make mistakes but they own up to it and make it right. They are held to a higher degree of accountability. Leaders must be responsible and express it. As the saying goes, the buck does indeed stop with you, the leader.

Your worth is not defined by likes, shares, retweets, nor numbers. Your worth is defined by the kindness and attention you authentically and so freely give.

Commitment 6

The Sixth Leadership Commitment
I will be an authentic leader.

I understand that authenticity is my greatest challenge, my greatest compliment, and my greatest gift to the world. While I add the wisdom of others to my life, I will not simply repeat what they have said or imitate what they have done. I will make each lesson my own. I will work to add my own unique contribution to the world. I will lead with integrity and a high moral standing. I will set high standards for myself and live up to them.

Leadership Takes Courage

You can accomplish anything! It's true.

Your life will not be determined by mere chance; it will be determined by your choices. Thank you for choosing to read this book. Whether you received *Along Came a Leader* as a gift, borrowed it from a friend, or purchased it yourself, I am glad you read it.

What is contained in these pages has the power to change your life and the lives of those around you. I know, because these ideas and principles have changed and enriched my life and those whom I love and with whom I spend my time.

Thank you for taking the courage to read this book. Apply what you have learned and encourage others to answer the call to lead.

The next time a challenge arises, and a leader is needed to *come along…* you will be ready and you will make a difference.

• • •

I have always wanted to meet a United States President. It was so much fun to meet and talk with President Bill Clinton. I will always remember him complimenting my tie. I asked President Clinton what was the most influential book he had ever read, and his answer really surprised me! President Clinton told me, the most influential book he had ever read was The Meditations of Marcus Aurelius.

The Six Leadership Commitments

Commitment 1

The First Leadership Commitment
I will lead with a great attitude.

I fully understand that my attitude is under my complete control. I understand the important correlation between leading and having a good, personal attitude. I will work daily on improving my attitude and the attitudes of those I lead.

Commitment 2

The Second Leadership Commitment
I will seek wisdom.

From this point forward, I will seek wisdom to become a better leader. I will read great books, surround myself with individuals who help me become a better leader, and I will reflect before I respond. I know wisdom is a continuing journey, and I will passionately pursue adding more wisdom to my leadership roles through a variety of sources.

Commitment 3

The Third Leadership Commitment
I will lead with tenacity.

Beginning today, I will enjoy the thrill of a challenge and lead with tenacity. I understand that I will face setbacks. I now know that a setback is simply an opportunity for a comeback and greater success. I will embrace the notion of falling down and getting back up. I will approach challenges with passion and see failures as stepping stones of success. I know I am a work in progress and am proud to be in a beta format. I know the only way I can truly fail is to quit, and I will not quit. I will lead with tenacity.

Commitment 4

The Fourth Leadership Commitment
I will consistently work at becoming a powerful communicator.

I will work from this point forward to master my ability to communicate. I fully understand the tight relationship between leading and communicating. I realize I am always communicating and will be more self-aware of the messages I am broadcasting as a leader.

Commitment 5

The Fifth Leadership Commitment
I will lead with an inspiring vision.

Knowing that vision is the guidance system of all leadership, I will create, embrace, and share an exciting and meaningful vision with my team often and with passion. I will help others see their role and contribution to the overall vision.

Commitment 6

The Sixth Leadership Commitment
I will be an authentic leader.

I understand that authenticity is my greatest challenge, my greatest compliment, and my greatest gift to the world. While I add the wisdom of others to my life I will not simply repeat what they have said or imitate what they have done. I will make each lesson my own. I will work to add my own unique contribution to the world. I will lead with integrity and a high moral standing.

Kelly Croy with Ohio Governor, Ted Strickland.

About the Author

K elly Croy resides in Oak Harbor, Ohio with his wife and four daughters. Kelly is a speaker, an artist and an educator.

www.KellyCroy.com

If you are interested in writing to the author, wish to receive his free newsletter, would like information about his speaking engagements, or would like to invite him to speak at an event you are hosting, please address all correspondence to:

Kelly Croy
218 East Main Street
Oak Harbor, Ohio 43449
United States of America
Phone: 1-800-831-4825

Kelly Croy

Email: info@kellycroy.com
www.kellycroy.com
www.Facebook.com/chalkart
www.twitter.com/kellycroy

Additional copies of
Along Came a Leader
are available on Kelly Croy's website:
www.KellyCroy.com
(Volume discounts available.)
or by calling:
1-800-831-4825

Acknowledgements

Richard Croy

I have dedicated this book to my father, Richard Croy, who passed away during the early writing of this manuscript. Several pages were drafted in Dad's hospital room, some of which I was able to share with Dad, and many that I could not due to the state of his health. Dad was the single greatest influence in my life in all areas, and especially in leadership. He encouraged me through the Boy Scouts, insisting I earn my Eagle Rank, and through sports, playing two collegiate sports and coaching for eighteen years. Dad really understood the principles of this book and not only taught them to me, but reinforced them in my life. Dad absolutely understood the idea of consistently improving in all areas. I wish to thank my dad for instilling the leadership qualities in me and encouraging me to always give my best in everything I do. I miss him greatly.

Patricia Croy

I absolutely must recognize and applaud my mother, who instilled in me discipline and faith. Her loving example of hard work, despite the hardships she faced, taught me how to live an honorable life. She has always been one of my greatest encouragers. Mothers are the most important leaders in this world, and my mother has been an incredible source of inspiration and leadership. While she is small in stature and soft spoken, she remains one of the most tenacious leaders I have ever met. She is absolutely unstoppable. Mothers do more to shape the minds and characters of our future CEOs, quarterbacks, legislators, surgeons, and innovators than anyone else. My mom, like all moms, is a leader in the home and in the community. She still inspires me today and holds me to the highest of standards. Thank you Mom for your example. Whatever success I have made in this world is a direct result of the parenting I received from my Mom and Dad.

Lorrain Croy

My wife is a source of great encouragement and my closest friend. She believes in me. All of the hours I spend writing and working on my art or presentations, have been for Lori and my four daughters, Allyson, Carolyne, Jaclyn, and Jillyan. I strive to be a better leader for these five women. After years of fiddling with my writing, Lori encouraged me to finish. She wants my stories and ideas down on paper, so if for no one else, I write for her. Lori is an amazing leader as well. She is an amazing attorney who daily demonstrates integrity and leadership inside and outside the courtroom. She comes home each night and helps lead our family of four daughters. Often during the writing of this book on leadership, I thought of how my wife lives the principles I wish to share with you in this volume. Lorrain Croy is a leader!

Dan Kalo

I had always heard the expression, "Once a Marine always a Marine," and now I know it to be true. Dan Kalo was a decorated Marine in the Vietnam War and the greatest man outside my father I have ever met. Dan gave me my first teaching job. I was only twenty-one and just out of college. He gave me an opportunity to teach and always held me to a higher standard. Dan taught me much about leadership. Dan is the epitome of loyalty, integrity, hard work, and character. I will always be indebted to this man. Every time I saw Dan, he made me stand an inch taller. He held everyone to the highest of standards and brought out the best within them. I miss him. Dan was like a second father to me. Dan Kalo was a great leader!

Gary Quisno

Gary is the greatest coach I have ever known. I am honored to have coached under him. He has become like a big brother to me. Gary taught me that you must devote time, real time, to your passions. He taught me the importance of becoming a student of my passions. He taught me the importance of developing a strong team and council. I admire Gary greatly. I am honored to call him friend.

Richard Baird

Rich is a great leader. He calls it like it is and he doesn't care what anyone thinks. He won't sugar-coat his response and he is fully focused on results. He cares for the forgotten, and gives so willingly and generously of his time and resources to all. I am so proud to have a friendship with this amazing leader.

Todd Moore

My longest friendship. He is truly like family. Our adventures as little boys have always spurred my interest in telling stories. Todd can figure anything out and never gives up. Somehow he taught that to me. There is always a solution. Always.

Del Culver

Every man deserves a friend like Del. I know that he will always be at my side despite the odds. He encourages me to become more every time we talk. He challenges me to take risks. He holds me accountable. He's a great listener. I can share anything with him. He knows how to have fun. I am constantly reminding myself to spend more time with Del.

Ty Roth

Ty is an author. Really. I am a wordsmith. Huge difference. I am so proud of his accomplishments. Ty's perseverance and success in the world of writing and publication has been a tremendous influence and education to me. I love talking with him about writing and literature. I hope to one day be half the writer Ty is today.

Tom Osborne

If I had written a chapter on intuition Tom would have been the focus. I have never met a man with such keen instincts in determing the characters and motives of others. Tom is a great friend and encourager. I have never met anyone as authentic as Tom. What you see is what you get. Tom is the most unpretentious man I have ever met.

Ben Glenn

I have always enjoyed art, writing, computers, music, and speaking. Ben showed me how to bring them all together. Thank you Ben for instructing me how to chalk and inspiring me to impact lives. Ben is the master chalk artist and speaker, and I am honored to have been his student. I admire Ben's faith, walk with God, and fun spirit. He impacted my life. I will always owe him a tremendous debt.

Chris Redfern

Chris is a man of action. He has taught me that leadership is about taking massive action to bring a vision to fruition and helping those in need. I have witnessed him making a difference in the lives of others through his actions as one of Ohio's greatest statesmen.

Frank Shelton

Meet him once and you will have a friend for life. Frank's phone calls, emails, faith, and words of encouragement are always a great joy to me. His encouragement to write this book was just the kick in the rear I needed. His guidance and tips along the way have been most helpful. Thank you Frank for inspiring me to excel with my speaking and art. Frank paved the way, showing me that completing my writing is possible.

Matthew Kelly

I have read Matthew's books, spent weekends with him at retreats, and have attended many of his performances. I appreciate his quick reply to all of my questions and his wisdom. He has truly become a friend and accountability partner. Matthew has been a tremendous influence on my writing, speaking and career. His generosity knows no bounds.

Justin Tank

I am very thankful for this former student from the earliest days of my teaching career. Justin volunteered to be an extra set of eyes in the proofreading of my book. He is a leader in the business world and in starting a new family, yet he took the time to help me with my manuscript. It is quite humbling to have a former student point out your errors, but it was greatly needed, and Justin did it with kindness and professionalism. I admire his entire family for their work ethic and strong values. I appreciate the encouragement from this next generation of leadership.

The Boy Scouts of America

The single greatest leadership decision I ever made in my life was to decide to work to become an Eagle Scout. I loved the camping trips and adventures. Scouting created my desire to become a teacher, and to become the best I could be at all I did. I wish more young men would become interested and committed to Scouting. It is one of the great resources of our country.

Football

To many football is a sport. To the men I played with and coached alongside, each season was more like a tour of duty in a war. Strategy, sacrifice, commitments of time, wins, losses, camaraderie, growth are all intricate parts of this amazing sport. The lessons about life, leadership, commitment, discipline, tenacity, sacrifice, competition, and camaraderie are abundant in quality football programs. I am so thankful to have been surrounded and led by incredible leaders in the sport. The impact they had on my life has opened countless doors.

U2

U2 has always been to me much more than a band. U2 is my muse. When I listen to their albums I am inspired to be more, do more, become more. Everyone should have a favorite band. Everyone should have a musical resource that inspires them. Though I listen to every genre of music for various reasons, U2 is my constant. U2 has done far more than make great music. They lead. They stand for something. They hold themselves accountable. They inspire. They yearn to make the world a better place. Their concerts are a spiritual experience for me, their albums medicine for my soul.

Quotes on Leadership

I really enjoy quotes. As a teacher, I write a new one on my classroom board every single day for my students. I use quotes often to meditate about a topic, and I use them to look inward at what I want to improve upon within my life. Great quotes, *when applied*, change lives. I have included some great ones here for you and throughout this book.

"Men make history, and not the other way around.
In periods where there is no leadership, society stands still.
Progress occurs when courageous, skillful leaders seize the
opportunity to change things for the better."
-Harry Truman

"You can begin to shape your own destiny by the attitude that you
keep."

~ Michael Beckwith

"It is our choices that show what we truly are, far more than our
abilities."

~J.K. Rowling

"You will never change your life until you change something you
do daily."

~John C. Maxwell.

Kelly Croy

"A leader is one who knows the way, goes the way, and shows the
way."

~John C. Maxwell

"Leaders must be tough enough to fight,
tender enough to cry,
human enough to make mistakes,
humble enough to admit them,
strong enough to absorb the pain,
and resilient enough to bounce back and keep on moving."

~Jesse Jackson

"If your actions inspire others to dream more, learn more, do more
and become more, you are a leader."

~John Quincy Adams

"Leadership can be thought of as a capacity to define oneself to
others in a way that clarifies and expands a vision of the future."

~Edwin H. Friedman

"I am a man of fixed and unbending principles, the first of which is
to be flexible at all times."

~Everett Dirksen

"Inventories can be managed, but people must be led."

~H. Ross Perot

"Whoever is providing leadership needs to be as fresh and

thoughtful and reflective as possible to make the very best fight."

~Faye Wattleton

"A community is like a ship; everyone ought to be prepared to take the helm."

~Henrik Ibsen

"I cannot give you the formula for success, but I can give you the formula for failure: which is: Try to please everybody."

~Herbert B. Swope

"A leader must have the courage to act against an expert's advice."

~James Callaghan

"You do not lead by hitting people over the head - that's assault, not leadership."

~Dwight D. Eisenhower

"There's nothing more demoralizing than a leader who can't clearly articulate why we're doing what we're doing."

~James Kouzes and Barry Posner

"Time is neutral and does not change things. With courage and initiative, leaders change things."

~Jesse Jackson

"Most important, leaders can conceive and articulate goals that lift people out of their petty preoccupations and unite them in pursuit of objectives worthy of their best efforts."

~John Gardner

"The key to successful leadership today is influence, not authority."

~Kenneth Blanchard

"I start with the premise that the function of leadership is to produce more leaders, not more followers."

~Ralph Nader

"Good leaders must first become good servants."

~Robert Greenleaf

"Effective leadership is putting first things first. Effective management is discipline, carrying it out."

~Stephen Covey

"The very essence of leadership is that you have to have a vision."

~Theodore Hesburgh

"Tis better to be silent and be thought a fool, than to speak and remove all doubt."

~Abraham Lincoln

"Do you want to know who you are? Don't ask. Act! Action will delineate and define you."

~Thomas Jefferson

"Do what you can, with what you have, where you are."

~ Theodore Roosevelt

"Change is the law of life. And those who look only to the past or present are certain to miss the future."

~John F. Kennedy

"You are not here merely to make a living. You are here in order to enable the world to live more amply, with greater vision, with a finer spirit of hope and achievement. You are here to enrich the world, and you impoverish yourself if you forget the errand."

~Woodrow Wilson

"Give me a stock clerk with a goal and I will give you a man who will make history. Give me a man without goals and I will give you a stock clerk."

~ J. C. Penny

"People forget how fast you did a job— but they remember how well you did it."

~Howard W. Newton

Meet and learn from leaders whenever you can. Kelly Croy with Jim Tressel and Hillary Clinton.

Leadership Maxims

- Leaders help to create a vision of what could be.
- Leaders reflect before making decisions.
- Leaders stand up and take action when others remain seated.
- Leaders ask questions when others remain silent.
- A leader says, "What if?" when everyone else is convinced nothing more can be done.
- A leader ignites a spark within us to become a better person and to do a little more.
- Leaders condition themselves not to be overly concerned with what others are thinking about them.
- A leader always takes action with the intent to help others and improve the situation.
- Leaders are constantly learning and improving themselves in all areas.
- A leader impacts the lives of others.
- Leaders learn the dreams of those around them and assists them on that journey.
- There is no job beneath a true leader.
- Leaders defend others when they know they are right.
- Leaders care about others.
- Leaders are good and kind.
- Leaders do not have double standards; they are fair.
- Leaders expect excellence from themselves and others.
- A leader is on a constant search for talent and resources.
- A leader takes risks.
- A leader confronts problems; preferably when they are small.
- Leaders enjoy the thrill of challenge.

- A leader's attitude influences the attitude of those around them.
- Leaders keep a journal.
- Leaders praise and recognize others meaningfully and frequently.
- Leaders are authentic; they act the same regardless of the social setting or environment.
- Leaders don't react, they respond.
- Leaders are confident.
- Leaders are visible.
- Leaders are able to confront others when they are wrong.
- Leaders avoid battles, but recognize the necessity to fight.
- Leaders help to create others leaders.
- Leaders do the extra work needed to make a difference, without being asked.

"Don't Judge each day by the harvest you reap, but by the seeds you plant."

~ Robert Louis Stevenson

If you are interested in writing to the author, wish to receive his free newsletter, would like information about his speaking engagements, or would like to invite him to speak at an event you are hosting, please address all correspondence to:

Kelly Croy
218 East Main Street
Oak Harbor, Ohio 43449
United States of America

Phone: 1-800-831-4825
Email: info@kellycroy.com
www.kellycroy.com

Additional copies of
Along Came a Leader
are available on Kelly Croy's website:
www.KellyCroy.com
(Volume discounts available.)
or by calling:
1-800-831-4825

The End.

Made in USA - Kendallville, IN
53244_9781512393064
07.26.2022 1325